Introduction

Robin Hartl

Dean Johnson

Like most home improvement projects, a tile job often starts with a file folder jammed full of pictures clipped from magazines. Looking over photos of beautiful tile jobs can inspire you to design a really outstanding installation, but it can also raise some doubts: Is it really possible for a do-it-yourselfer to accomplish an intricate tile installation and will it hold up over time?

The answer is yes. With research, planning, thought, and practice, all aspects of a tilesetting job can be mastered by amateurs. While there are no great mysteries to tilesetting, we do have an important tip: If you want a professional-looking job, you have to spend some time doing the prep work. Think, plan, ask questions, think some more, plan some more, do part of the job, think some more, ask some more questions – you get the idea.

Once you get to the actual tilesetting, the job usually breaks down into small, manageable jobs – underlayment, layout, field tile, accent tile, grouting, caulking – that allow you to take your time and do it right. You can spread it out over many evenings or a couple of weekends unless, of course, you're tiling around your only bathtub. In that case you might want to dig in and just get the job done!

Table of Contents

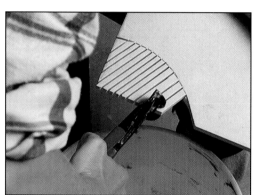

CERAMIC TILE
How to

Real People – Real Projects®

HOMETIME®

Publisher: Dean Johnson
Editor: Pamela S. Price
Writers: John Kelsey, Laura Tringali
Art Director: Bill Nelson
Associate Editor: Jason Adair
Copy Editor: Lisa Wagner

Hometime Hosts: Dean Johnson, Robin Hartl
Project Producer: Matt Dolph
Construction and Technical Review: Chris Balamut, Wade Barry, Mark Kimball, Dan Laabs, Judd Nelson
Production Crew: Tom (Buki) Weckwerth, Mark Gutzmer, Scott Burdick

Illustrator: Mario Ferro
Photographer: Jeff Lyman
Cover Photo: Maki Strunc Photography
Electronic Imaging: Jennifer S. Parks

Production Coordinator: Pam Scheunemann
Electronic Layout: M. Elizabeth Salzmann

Book Creative Direction, Design, and Production: MacLean & Tuminelly, Minneapolis, MN
Cover Design: Richard Scales Advertising

Electronic Prepress: Encore Color Group
Printed by: RR Donnelley & Sons Co.
Printed in the United States

5 4 3 2 1 / 03 02 01 00 99

Library of Congress Catalog Card Number 98-75328
ISBN 1-890257-05-2

HOMETIME®
4275 Norex Drive
Chaska, MN 55318

Special Thanks: Jim Way, A to Z Rental; Cynthia and Rick Anderson; Marlene Jackson, Aqua Mix, Inc.; Teri and Curt Benson; Douglas Carlson, Country Floors & Tile; J.D. Kressel, Dennis Oliver, Cutting Edge Tile; Linda Morrison, Florida Tile; Kathi Johnson; Doug Krumlauf; Carol Ward, Laufen Ceramic Tile; Ron Williamson, Metropolitan Ceramics; Jay Switzer, Kimberly Stahura, Bob Kietzman, Minnesota Tile Supply; Susan Price and Noah Tant; Peter Price and Julie Whitney; Jerry Thompson; Bruce Shapiro and Bev Trombley; Sharon Zukley, TEC, Inc.; Janet VanFossan

Contributing Photography: Country Floors & Tile, Laufen Ceramic Tile

The procedures featured in this book are for people with average home repair and improvement skills. If you are inexperienced in the use of any applicable tools, materials, or equipment, or if you're uncertain whether the procedures shown or described are appropriate for your specific situation, consult a skilled professional *before* you begin work.

Follow all manufacturer instructions for the use of tools and materials, and seek the manufacturers' advice if the instructions in this book deviate from manufacturers' use-and-care guidelines. The publisher disclaims any liability for injury or damage resulting from the use of tools, materials, or procedures included in this book. Proper use of equipment and products is your responsibility, and your performance is at your own risk.

Our materials and procedures are based on common practice and the Uniform Building Code (UBC) which prevailed at the time this book was written. Local regulations *may vary* from the UBC, and the UBC may also change periodically. *Always* check relevant local regulations and obtain necessary permits before starting work.

For online project help and information on other Hometime products, visit us on the Web at **www.hometime.com**

PLANNING and DESIGN

The minute you set foot in the tile section of a home center or walk through the doors of a tile showroom, you'll be dazzled by the design possibilities offered by tile. It comes in so many colors, shapes, styles, and sizes that anything and everything seems possible. But your initial excitement can soon turn to frustration and confusion as you try to narrow your choices to what's right for your budget and tilesetting skills – not to mention the style of your home.

The answer to this dilemma is simple: Do your homework. Figure out what you can spend and what style of tile will best suit your home. To guide your choices, clip pictures of tile jobs that you like, but leave your mind open to new possibilities. Then, have fun shopping.

Where to Use Tile

Ceramic tile has always been at home in bathrooms and kitchens, but its versatility also makes it a top choice for entries, hallways, and sunrooms. As an accent material, it enhances surfaces from fireplace surrounds to door and window trim.

Floors

A properly installed ceramic tile floor offers durability, easy cleaning (some tile styles even hide dirt), and water resistance. On the downside, a tile floor can chill bare feet in winter and stress your back and legs if you stand on it for a long time.

Floor tiles fall into three main groups: glazed tiles, quarry tiles, and pavers. A glazed floor tile is any glazed tile strong enough to stand up to heavy use. Quarry tiles resemble quarried stone, but are made from clay. Pavers are made either by hand or machine from clay, shale, or porcelain. They may be glazed or unglazed. Since hand-made pavers are fired at a low temperature, they absorb more water than other types of tile, making them a poor choice for wet areas.

Unglazed tiles should be sealed to prevent stains from soaking in; glazed tiles are stain-resistant, but the glaze can scratch unless you buy a tile with a durable finish or one that won't show scratches easily.

If the floor will be exposed to water, you need to buy tiles that won't become slippery when wet. Many floor tiles have rough, slip-resistant finishes to help prevent accidents.

Countertops

Glazed floor tiles make the best countertop surfaces because they can stand up to hot cookware and sharp utensils. For easy cleaning, any tile installed on a countertop should have a smooth surface. Never select unglazed tiles

The small hexagonal floor tiles shown here are less slippery than the high-gloss green tiles – important in a shower. Note the way the green tiles are positioned in different patterns on the horizontal and vertical surfaces. This, along with the white tiles, keeps the green from becoming overwhelming. Tiling right up to the ceiling eliminates the need for bullnose and other trim tiles.

A new ceramic tile countertop and floor add warmth and life to this contemporary-style kitchen. The light-colored 12x12 floor tiles make the room seem more spacious. To prevent cracks from developing, large tiles like these must be set on a flat base.

for a countertop because they stain easily. What's more, the protective sealers that make them stain-resistant are not recommended for use around food.

Walls

Ceramic wall tiles are thinner than floor tiles and have a thinner glaze, but they're anything but fragile. Typically, wall tiles are 4- or 6-inch squares, although it's easy to find other sizes. To make installation easier, very small wall tiles sometimes come mounted on sheets of paper, plastic, or mesh fabric.

While you can use floor tiles on a wall, you'll need a strong adhesive to hold the heavier floor tiles. Another thing to consider: Floor tiles usually don't have matching trim pieces.

Thin-sliced natural materials (such as the brown marble shown here) are attractive, but expensive. If you like the look, but not the price tag, look for ceramic tiles that resemble natural materials – they're a fraction of the cost. It's important to dry-lay stone and stone-look tiles so you can blend the colors evenly over the floor.

Cleaning glazed tile is simply a matter of whisking away spills, drips, and mud with a rag or sponge – that's why it's great for high-traffic areas. To remain stain-free, porous unglazed tiles and grout must be sealed with silicone sealer.

The great outdoors

Ceramic tiles are primarily used indoors, but they're also ideal for patios, walkways, and pool decks, as long as they have a skid-resistant surface to provide traction in wet weather. Typically the tile is set in a mortar bed over a 3-inch thick slab of concrete. If it's in relatively good shape, it's possible to give an existing concrete patio a tile facelift.

Until recently, outdoor tile installations were not an option in cold-climate areas. However, there are now tiles, adhesives, and grouts that can stand up to repeated freeze/thaw cycles.

Glass or ceramic kitchenware is likely to break if dropped on a ceramic tile floor or counter. Families with small children should use plastic dishes and cups – or be prepared for frequent breakage.

Designing with Tile

With ceramic tile you can create looks that range from high-tech to rustic, depending on the color, size, and style of the tiles you choose. Tile alone doesn't create the whole effect, though. Grout color, joint size, and the tile layout all contribute to the overall look of the job.

An accent band of tumbled marble adds drama to a ceramic tile wall. It's easier to install than it looks since the tiles are backed with mesh strips. The built-in shelf (made of solid-surface material) is less expensive than stone shelves.

Color

Until recently, the trend in tile color was toward the neutrals: white, almond, and gray. Now more people are beginning to experiment with bright colors. If you're using a variety of colors in a project (or even a single strong color), buy or borrow at least a few square feet of the tile and live with it for a few days. Make sure you like the tile before you invest your time and money.

If your budget is limited, a few colorful accent tiles inserted here and there can perk up a field of inexpensive white tiles.

Shape

Straight-edged rectangular or square tiles are probably most popular tile shapes, but you can find tiles in more exotic shapes. Some, like Moorish and ogee tiles, are curvy; there's also an elongated, slightly rounded hexagon shape called a key hexagon. Mosaics come in pebble styles as well as the more typical square, rectangular, and hexagonal shapes.

Light-colored tiles make a space seem brighter, but they also show dirt and require more cleaning. The swirls and streaks in this tile add depth and texture without compromising the airy feel.

Dark tiles can visually shrink a space or make it seem cozy and welcoming, depending on your personal taste. Light-colored fixtures and accessories help balance intense colors.

Grout

It's easy to overlook grout as a design element, but both grout color and the width of the grout joints visibly affect the project. Matching the grout color to the color of the tile blends the two materials and helps hide any variations in tile height or size, as well as uneven tile spacing. Using a dark grout with a light tile, or vice versa, will emphasize the geometric pattern of your layout – and the layout better be perfect because the contrast will call attention to anything that is not. If you do decide to go wild with a colored grout, test it in a small area first.

Avoid using light-colored grout on floors that get heavy traffic from outdoors because it's difficult to keep clean. Gray is a traditional grout color – it hides dirt and goes well with many colors of tile, especially natural stone and terra cotta tiles.

The width of the grout joints is almost as important as color. While personal preference plays a large part here, tradition dictates that grout joints should be kept in rough proportion to tile size. While you could go up to ⅜ inch on large tiles, keep in mind that the larger the joint, the more prone it is to cracking.

Pattern

One way to jazz up a tile installation is with a patterned layout. Even plain white tile takes on an elegant appearance when set on the diagonal. However, keep in mind that diagonal, herringbone, and running bond

As this ribbon pattern unfurls elegantly across the floor, it adds the illusion of depth to the flat tiled surface. A design this complex requires many cuts and must be worked out very carefully on paper first.

Grout that contrasts with the tile color is more noticeable than grout that matches. Whether that's good or bad is a matter of personal preference. Here, using dark grout (left) with mostly light-colored tile emphasizes the strong geometrics of the design. Grouting the same tiles with a light-colored grout (right) softens the impact of the floor considerably.

Changing the width of the grout joints dramatically changes the look of the tile. Wider joints look more rustic, narrower joints more formal. Also, narrower joints emphasize the tile more than wider joints. Joint size is a matter of personal taste, but keep in mind that the wider the grout joint, the more likely it will be to crack.

patterns are harder to install than straight-line patterns. They require more layout lines and more cuts along the edges. Also, more cuts means more waste, so patterned layouts will increase your budget slightly.

Color can also be used to create pattern in a layout. Choices range from simple checkerboards to complex crazy-quilt designs. Of course, patterns based on square or rectangular shapes will be easier to create than ones requiring irregular-shaped tiles. It's also simpler to keep the design on track if you stick to just two or three colors.

Large limestone wall tiles combine nicely with tumbled marble floor tiles in this shower stall. The light colors of both tiles tie everything together, but there's just enough contrast to make it visually interesting. The built-in shower bench is made of two limestone tiles glued together.

Size

Tile comes in a vast array of sizes. While the standard 4-inch square wall tile is still the most popular, the current trend is toward larger floor tiles, like 8x8s, 10x10s, 12x12s, and even 16x16s.

Conventional wisdom holds that it's best to use large tiles in large rooms and small tiles in small rooms. This, however, is a matter of taste – go with what looks best to you.

Small 1-inch tiles (called mosaics) are also common. You can mix different colors to create borders, patterns, and pictures. These tiles are usually joined together in 12x12 or 12x24 sheets to make them easier and faster to set.

Texture

Texture is added to a tile by manipulating either the glaze or the clay. If you like the look, floor tiles with a textured glaze offer better traction than slick-glazed tiles. They also help hide dirt – a big plus, since they're often harder to clean. Glaze can also be used to create the appearance of texture where there is none. For example, several colors of glaze applied to a flat ceramic tile can make it look like a rough-cut stone tile.

Simple textures are added to tile by etching the clay before the tile is fired. You'll find everything from simple lines and cross-hatches to complex patterns. Handmade artisan tiles often feature relief patterns ranging from simple geometric patterns to detailed animal figures. Because of their cost, these are generally used only as accent tiles and in places they are sure to be noticed, such as wall borders and backsplashes. Texture can also be added to the clay unintentionally; the handmade tiles crafted in Mexico or the Mediterranean sometimes have animal tracks or finger marks in them.

Large tiles work best in large rooms, as a rule of thumb. When a smaller tile is used in a large room, it changes the character of the space dramatically. To some people, large tiles make a small room look even smaller; others may think small tiles make the room look smaller (since additional grout lines add visual clutter).

Many tile lines include *practical and sometimes whimsical accent and trim pieces, such as this tree-branch-shaped towel hook. When shopping for wall tile, don't forget to check what matching accessory pieces are offered. If there isn't enough variety, you may want to switch to another line.*

Tiles can be easily arranged *into a variety of geometric patterns to bring personality and a custom look to any job. Work out your pattern carefully on paper first. The built-in shower shelf shown here (made from limestone) is an elegant accent.*

Only a professional *(or an experienced D-I-Yer with unlimited patience and time) should attempt to tackle a pattern as elaborate as this one. If your ability isn't up to this level of work, don't worry. Other stunning effects are within the range of even novice tilesetters.*

When you shop for tile, take a sketch of the room to be tiled, along with accurate measurements. Also bring the pictures you've clipped from magazines, paint chips, and fabric swatches. Tile showrooms often feature displays of tiles in actual settings, so it's a good idea to take along a camera so you can snap pictures of designs that you like. Look over your options carefully, jotting down notes on colors, styles, and available trim pieces.

Bring home sample tiles so you can make your final selection in the room where the tile will be installed. Most tile dealers will loan you samples for a day or two. Hold the tiles against cabinets, woodwork, and furniture to see how each fits in with your decor.

Backsplashes

There's no simpler way to add a bit of your own personality to a kitchen than with a tile backsplash. You can use a tile backsplash with any counter-top material – tile, plastic laminate, or solid-surface. If the counter isn't tiled, you'll get maximum effect by installing the backsplash tiles all the way from the counter to the bottom of the upper cabinets, but even a single row of tile can perk up a kitchen or bath. And since they're typically used on a fairly small wall area, you can splurge on fancy decorator tiles without breaking the bank.

When choosing tiles for a short backsplash, consider using self-trimming tiles, such as bullnose tiles or quarter-round trim tiles, for the top row. Or, check to see if your tile manufacturer offers any eye-catching trim tiles. Many tile lines feature striking accent pieces that you can use to cap off the top of the backsplash.

The fruit motif of this backsplash complements the red kitchen sink. With any backsplash, it's important to keep the grout lines straight and even. Where the grout contrasts with colorful tiles, extra care will be required both in aligning the tiles and applying the grout.

Even a simple backsplash such as this one can be visually effective, especially when capped with contrasting trim. The backsplash extends up the wall over the range to take advantage of the easy cleanup tile offers.

Same tile, different effect. Here, the colorful fruit tiles seen at left are set off by black rope trim tiles. Running the black and white checkerboard pattern in the backsplash and along the countertop edge ties the two together visually.

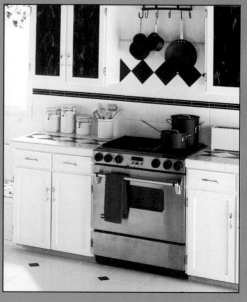

TOOLS
and MATERIALS

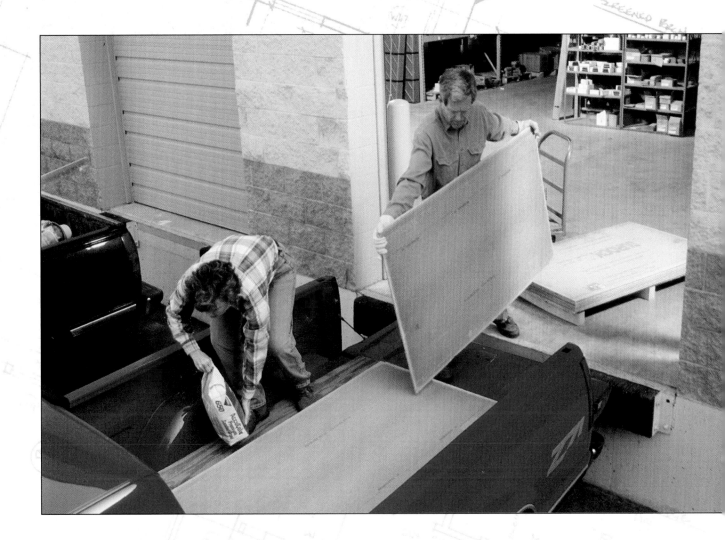

Whether the installation is simple or complex, *classic or exotic, the tiles are the focal point of the project. However, selecting tools and materials for your job deserves careful attention, too. Backer board may not be much to look at, but it's a key part of most tiling projects, providing a stable, sturdy base for the tile. Likewise, the proper adhesive and grout can make all the difference to the life span of your tile job. As for tools, there is no better way to sabotage a job than by using dull, make-do equipment. For each task that is required to make your tile installation come out right, there is probably a tool that will do the job quickly and efficiently. It pays to take a little time to find out which tools you'll need before you start working. Most aren't expensive and the ones that are, such as specialized saws and tile-cutting equipment, can usually be rented.*

Tile

Ceramic tiles are made from various clays and other minerals. After they're shaped, they're fired in a kiln at a high temperature. The resulting tile, called a bisque, can either be left natural or finished with a glaze. The glaze is typically fused to the bisque under high heat.

The strength and durability of a ceramic tile depends on the type of clay that was used to make it. Clay containing few air pockets produces a dense bisque, while bisque made from clay with lots of air pockets is less dense. Density affects water absorption. Obviously, when tiling an area in wet or splash-prone settings, it makes sense to use a denser material that absorbs little or no water (vitreous and impervious tiles) than one that will soak it up (nonvitreous and semi-vitreous tiles). When shopping, don't be surprised to find out that impermeable tiles cost more than permeable tiles.

Mosaic tiles are available in many sizes of squares, octagons, and hexagons, as well as in special designs. The smaller sizes are mounted on mesh sheets for easier installation. Many mosaics are made of porcelain.

Types of ceramic tile

Tiles are grouped in the store by use – wall, floor, or counter – but this labeling system doesn't tell the whole story. What you also need to know is just how absorbent a tile is. Just because a tile is rated strong enough for floors, for example, doesn't necessarily mean that it will stand up to the water and dirt tracked into a mudroom.

Professional tile-setters talk about absorbency in terms of vitreousness. Tiles may be (in order of decreasing absorbency) nonvitreous, semi-vitreous, vitreous, or impervious. For that mudroom floor, you would probably want to use a semi-vitreous or vitreous floor tile.

Manufacturers may also specify a tile's absorbency as a percentage of its weight.

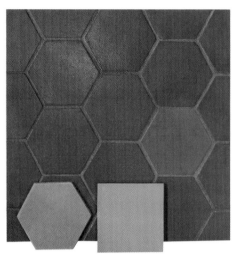

Terra cotta tiles can be made either by hand or by machine. They come in a variety of sizes, and vary in color, texture, and appearance.

Porcelain tiles are smooth and impervious. Because the color runs all the way through the bisque, chips and scratches aren't very noticeable.

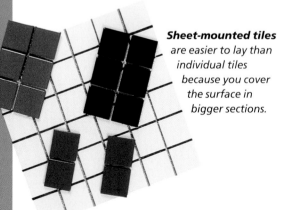

Sheet-mounted tiles are easier to lay than individual tiles because you cover the surface in bigger sections.

Stone tiles may be made of slate, granite, limestone, or plain or tumbled marble. They're usually more expensive than ceramic tiles.

Saltillo tiles, often referred to as Mexican tiles, are handmade and come in a range of earth-tone colors. Since they're porous even when sealed, keep them away from wet areas.

Quarry tiles can be glazed or unglazed, made from natural clay or shale. Many quarry tiles are dark red, but gray and brown shades are also available. All are machine made.

They take more work and consume more energy to produce, and this is reflected in the price.

Not all tiles are made from clay. Stone tiles are either cut and polished to precise dimensions or split from the stone in somewhat irregular slices, offering a variety of different looks and characteristics. Marble, for example, makes a stunning floor and, while it scratches easily, dings can usually be buffed out. Although stone tiles are slightly harder to cut, they're set using standard tiling methods.

Tile finishes

Glazes protect and decorate ceramic tiles, but not all glazes are created equal. A glaze fired at a lower temperature and for fewer hours will be less durable than one that's been fused to the tile by a long, hot stay in the kiln. How do you tell? Check the manufacturer's specifications to find out if a tile is rated for use on walls, floors, or countertops. Beyond this, you can take a sample tile home and put it to the test: Grind your heel into a tile to get a measure of its scuff-resistance. Drop a few things on it to see how resistant it is to chipping. This is important: Since the color stops with the glaze, any chips and scratches will expose the clay base underneath. (The exception is porcelain tiles, which have color all the way through.)

Some glazes contain materials that add texture to the finish. Some, such as sawdust, burn off in the kiln, while others, including sand or silica, remain in the glaze. While textured surfaces are more skid-resistant than perfectly smooth ones, they can still be somewhat slippery when wet. Where good traction is critical, consider slate, limestone, or even brick-veneer tiles instead.

The back of a ceramic tile often is finished with raised dots, crosshatches, or ridges. Mostly these provide more surface for the adhesive to grab on to, although some are added just because they make it easier to stack the tiles for firing.

Glossy glazes reflect light and can make small spaces look larger. They're also easy to clean. Wear marks and scratches will be noticeable, so use high-gloss tiles in somewhat protected areas.

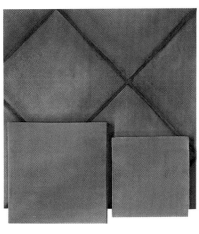

Unglazed tiles *should be sealed with a silicone sealer to keep them from staining. They should be sealed before grouting (so the grout doesn't stain the tile), and then about once a year as the sealer wears off.*

The glaze on wall tiles *is usually softer than and not as scratch-resistant as the glazes applied to floor and countertop tiles.*

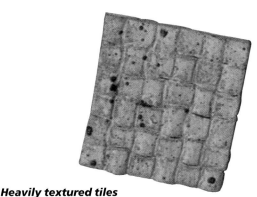

Heavily textured tiles *look great on their own, or they can be used as accent pieces when set in a field of plain tiles. They can also be used to create a frame around an area of smooth-surfaced tiles.*

Tumbled marble tiles
*are ideal for use on walls,
counters, bars, and shower
floors, and to accent ceramic
tile floors. You can also use
them as the primary tile,
although this is expensive.
The natural, almost
bleached, colors of tum-
bled marble come in pastels
as well as earth tones.
The rounded
corners
give them
a softer,
aged look.*

Specialty tiles

Specialty tiles are functional works of art.
Handmade artisan tiles may feature intricate
painted designs or relief patterns. Because of
their expense, it's best to use artisan tiles on
vertical surfaces where they'll receive less
wear and tear – and where it's easier to see
and admire them. One-of-a-kind art tiles
from local artisans are often available from
tile showrooms; check with several to get the
complete picture of what's available.

Many manufacturers also produce specialty
tiles to complement their standard tile lines.
These tiles are available at tile showrooms and
well-stocked home centers. No matter where
you buy them, specialty tiles aren't cheap.
To save money, use specialty tiles sparingly –
perhaps scattering them here and there
throughout a field of mass-produced tiles or
to artfully cap off an installation.

*Relief
tiles made
of terra
cotta have
long been
used to add
architectural
detail. They are
made all over
the world.*

Moldings

Moldings and ropes
are often used as
accent tiles near the
top of a project, some-
times in combination
with bullnose tiles.
They come in many
patterns, featuring a
variety of motifs in
styles ranging from
Victorian to Art Deco
and contemporary.

Some hand-painted tiles *are made to fit together to create a larger design. Since hand-
painted tiles are expensive, using them to create a
picture in a field of solid-color tile is a good way to
make the most of your budget.*

Tiles with printed or stenciled *designs (center
and right) are a more affordable alternative to
tiles that are painted by hand (left). Because they
look hand painted, you can get a very similar
effect for a very different price.*

Adhesives

The type of adhesive you use depends on where you're tiling and what you're tiling on. You have two basic choices: thinset mortars or organic mastics.

Thinset mortar

Thinset comes in powder form and must be mixed on site. You can make it stronger and more water-resistant by using liquid latex or acrylic (instead of water) to mix the thinset. However, some thinsets come with powdered latex or acrylic already added – mix these with water only. Check with your supplier to make sure you're getting the right mix of products.

Thinset is tricky to work with because it must be mixed to the right consistency before use, but it creates a superior bond and is more flexible when cured than mastic. It can also support a lot of weight, so it's often used for floor installations. Since thinset is more water-resistant than mastic, it's recommended for use in wet areas. If you are setting tiles with thinset and will be using a light-colored grout, consider using a light-colored thinset. This way the thinset will be less visible through the grout.

Organic mastics

Mastics are probably the adhesives most commonly used by do-it-yourself tilesetters; maybe it's because they come premixed. Mastics also make it much easier to set wall tiles because they have a stronger immediate grip on the tile than thinset. While most pros stick with thinset for walls as well as floors because of its superior strength, flexibility, and water-resistance, we've had good luck setting wall tiles with mastic. Just be sure to get a mastic formulated for wet areas if you're tiling a shower or tub surround.

Mastics are available in water-based or solvent-based mixes. If you use a solvent-based mastic, be sure to wear an organic-vapor respirator when working, keep the mastic well away from open flames, and ventilate the room.

Thinset powder is added to the liquid, then mixed by hand or with a paddle chucked into a ½-inch drill. It should be mixed to the consistency of thick, stiff mud, then left to slake for ten minutes before giving it a final stir. Only mix up as much as you can use in about 30 minutes.

The notched edge of the trowel is used to comb ridges in the adhesive. Adhesive manufacturers specify the type and size of notch needed to provide the right coverage for a good bond with the tile.

Liquid latex or acrylic additives add strength to the thinset. Sometimes they're already in the mix and you just have to add water. If not, mix the powder using the additive in place of water. Pour the additive into a large bucket, then add the thinset powder a little at a time, stirring frequently.

Spacers and wedges

For straight, uniform grout lines, you'll need to keep consistent spacing between tiles. Most wall tiles have spacing lugs built in, while most floor tiles don't. Although you can use plastic spacers between your floor tiles, we prefer to rely on a grid of reference lines, a story pole, and our eyes – if the spacing looks good, it is good. However, when setting wall tiles, we do use plastic wedges to help hold the trim tiles (which don't have spacer lugs) in place until the adhesive has set.

Underlayment

Because ceramic tile is rigid and somewhat brittle, a strong flat underlayment is fundamental to a successful tile job. You have several options:

Cement backer board

Backer board is probably the best option for D-I-Y tilesetters. It's typically made from a solid cement core faced with fiberglass skins, but other types of backer board (primarily fiber-cement products) are now common. Both types are unaffected by moisture and can be used for floors, walls, and countertops in wet or dry areas. Backer board panels come in a variety of sizes and in thicknesses of ¼, ⁵⁄₁₆, ½, and ⅝ inch.

Plywood

Exterior-grade plywood underlayment can be used for floors and countertops, although backer board is the better choice if it's available. On floors, the plywood must be installed over an adequate subfloor – the two together should measure no less than 1⅛ inches thick. Substrates for countertops are typically made up of a layer of ¾-inch exterior-grade plywood topped with backer board. In high-moisture areas, tilesetters often install a rubber membrane over a wood underlayment. This helps to protect the wood from moisture and to isolate the tile from movement in the wood caused by fluctuations in temperature and humidity.

Drywall

Drywall makes a good underlayment for wall tile in areas that won't be exposed to moisture. Moisture-resistant drywall (often called greenboard) used to be the underlayment of choice in wet areas, but may no longer be acceptable in some places and situations for use as a tile underlayment. In cold climates you may not be allowed to use greenboard on exterior walls because of moisture and vapor barrier issues. Check with your local building department to be sure you're using the right product.

Mud beds

Professional tilesetters sometimes float a mortar, or mud, bed as an underlayment. Installing a mud bed requires expert masonry skills. If your job requires a mud bed (perhaps because of a weak or uneven subfloor), hire a tile contractor to install it.

Tiling over existing floors

Existing ceramic tile or vinyl flooring are acceptable underlayments for new tile if they are in good condition. If the flooring is cushioned vinyl or linoleum, or if there is more than one layer of flooring, you'll need to remove it and install a new underlayment. Since older resilient flooring may contain asbestos, don't pull it up without first having it evaluated by a test lab. Flooring containing asbestos can either be covered over or removed by an abatement professional.

Never tile directly over wooden plank flooring. It has too much flex – you'll have cracked tiles in no time at all.

Concrete slabs and masonry walls are good substrates for tile if they're flat, clean, and have no structural cracks. (Concrete surfaces with small nonstructural cracks should be covered with an isolation membrane before tiling.) However, some adhesives can't be used over concrete, so consult your dealer before you buy.

The combination of subfloor, underlayment, and thinset mortar makes a solid base for a tile floor. All these layers, plus the tile, add to the height of the finished floor, so consider how that will affect doors, plumbing fixtures, appliances, cabinets, wood trim, and adjacent floors before finalizing your plan. Note the similarity of the underlayment construction for floors and countertops. In dry areas or areas that won't typically get soaked with water, wall tiles can be directly attached to the existing drywall (provided it's in good condition). Switch to backer board for an underlayment in wet areas.

Grout

There are two types of grout used for most tile jobs – sanded and unsanded. Both types come powdered and can be mixed with an acrylic or latex additive to make the grout stronger, easier to spread, less prone to shrinkage, and more moisture resistant. That last point is important. While grout does prevent water from flowing directly into the joints between tiles, it is not waterproof. Standing water can seep through grout into the substrate below.

Grout is available in an assortment of colors, and most grout manufacturers also make caulks in matching colors. Color-matched caulks are available sanded and unsanded to match the texture of the grout.

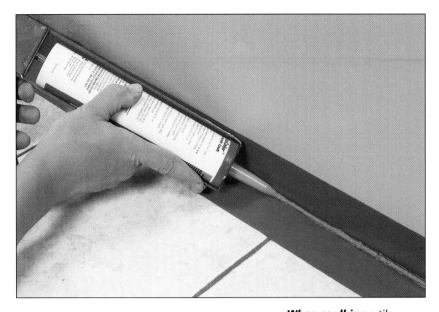

When caulking a tile installation, use either a clear tub/shower caulk or one in a color that matches the grout, as shown here. Use caulk, not grout, wherever the tile meets other materials and where tiles meet on two planes.

Use sanded grout for joints wider than ⅛ inch. The sand adds strength and helps prevent cracked grout joints. Sanded grout that is rated for wider joints has larger grains of sand.

Unsanded grout is best suited for joints less than ⅛ inch wide. It's easier to work than sanded grout, especially when you're grouting small mosaic tiles.

Grout-sample kits allow you to see how different colors of grout will look with your tile. Since different manufacturers offer different grout colors, if you don't find a good match with one manufacturer, keep looking.

Grout sealer helps keep the grout from absorbing water and becoming stained by dirt and mildew. Use a brush when sealing sanded grout – its rough texture can shred foam applicators.

This tool will help you to accurately transfer the layout of your tiles from paper to the tiling surface. To make one, take a good, straight 1x4 and mark it with the width of the tiles and grout joint; since size can vary from tile to tile as well as box to box, take the average of several tiles to get a true size.

Helpful layout tools
include (from top to bottom) a story pole, a 24-inch level, and a framing square. You'll also need a calculator, a pencil, a retractable measuring tape that's at least 25 feet long, and a chalk line to snap long, straight layout lines.

Tools

The tools for tilesetting are pretty basic, and you probably already have many of them. All but a few of the specialized tools are readily available and fairly inexpensive to purchase. You can rent the expensive equipment, such as a snap cutter or wet saw, from your tool-rental company or tile dealership. Some suppliers will loan you the tools you need if you buy all your materials from them – it doesn't hurt to ask. If you rent, check that the edge of the saw or cutter you'll be using is sharp and sound before you leave the rental store. Ask how to use the tool if you don't know how, and be sure that all safety guards are in place.

Because ceramic tile is extremely hard and brittle, you'll need to use special blades and bits when drilling or cutting it with power tools. Drill bits should be carbide-tipped, and saw blades should be labeled as the type designed specifically for cutting ceramic tile.

Clean your tools right away to avoid having to spend money on replacements. Once hardened, adhesives and grouts are almost impossible to remove.

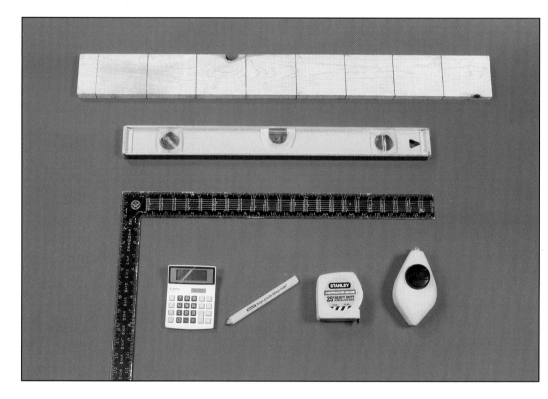

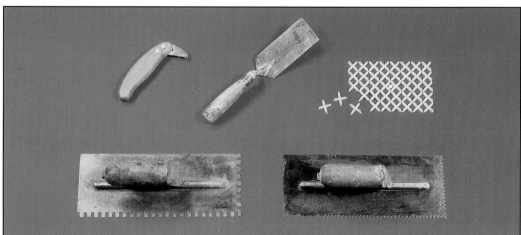

For setting tile, *you'll need (top row) a backer board scoring knife, a margin trowel to mix up mortar and grout, and plastic spacers (if you decide to use them). Use notched trowels (bottom row) to spread adhesive: square-notched for thinset, V-notched for mastic.*

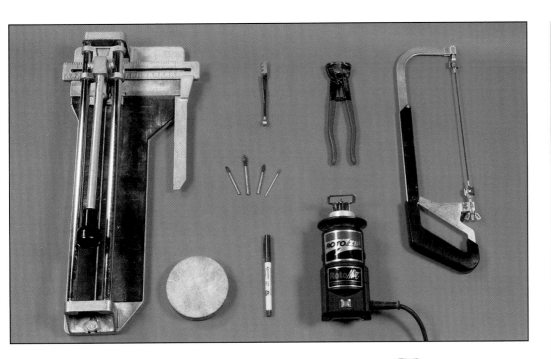

Specialized cutting tools (clockwise from left: a snap cutter, glass cutter, tile nipper, rod saw, spiral saw, rub stone, and carbide-tipped drill bits) let you handle just about any type of tile cut. The snap cutter scores a straight cutline, then snaps the tile in two. For irregular cuts, use nippers or a rod saw – of the two, the rod saw leaves a cleaner edge. A wet saw (right) is the most efficient way to make straight cuts with clean, smooth edges – rent one if you have lots of cuts to make. Wet saws spray water around, so set it up outside or in the garage.

For grouting, you'll need a padded grout float (left) to work the grout into the joints. You'll also need a bucket, grout sponge, and soft rags for cleanup, and rubber gloves to protect your hands.

Safety gear

Safety gear recommended for tiling jobs includes goggles and particulate respirators to protect your eyes and lungs when you're cutting tile and mixing powdered thinset or grout. Add hearing protectors when cutting tile with power tools.

To protect your skin, wear heavy gloves for demolition and rubber gloves when working with thinset or grout (wet cement products are caustic). Finally, don't forget kneepads. Tile is hard, and kneeling on it – or worse yet, on tile shards – can cause serious pain.

The first step in calculating the amount of floor tile you'll need is to measure the area to be covered. Break up odd-shaped rooms into manageable rectangles, squares, and triangles, figure the square footage individually (in case you've forgotten, the area of a right-angle triangle is ½ width x height), then add them together. Subtract the square footage of an island or peninsula from your total.

Buying extra

Before you buy your tile, multiply the estimated amount by 5 to 10 percent. Stay to the higher percentage if your layout has a fancy pattern or requires lots of cuts. Add that percentage to the estimate to figure the total amount of tile that you should buy. The extra will cover breakage and the waste you'll inevitably generate as you cut whole tiles to fit. Be sure to also buy some extra tiles that you can stockpile for future repairs.

Estimating

The ideal estimate gives you enough tile to do the project, compensates for waste and breakage, and leaves a few tiles to store for future repairs as needed. Estimating a job that will be covered with the same size and color of tile is relatively easy: Just divide the area of the project by the area of a single tile plus the width of one grout joint. This tells you roughly the number of tiles needed.

To figure the number of tiles you'll need, divide the square footage of the installation by the area of one tile plus the width of a grout joint. To stay organized, keep a checklist of things to buy or rent.

When the tiles are irregularly shaped, lay out a small area of tile to figure out how many tiles will fit into one square foot. Multiply this number by the overall square footage to determine the total tiles needed.

To estimate adhesive, compare the square footage of the area to be tiled with the coverage specifics on the container. (Most labels specify their coverage areas using various trowel and tile sizes.) Get as close as you can without being tight – it's always better to have a bit too much than too little.

Grout can be confusing to estimate at first. The box should indicate pounds of grout needed for a range of surface areas, tile sizes, and grout-joint widths. When in doubt, ask for help.

In any case, when you purchase your materials, ask your retailer if you will be able to return unopened boxes of tile or bags of mortar and grout at the end of the project.

TILING BASICS

Simple or complex, the steps in a tile job pretty much follow the same sequence. You prepare a flat, sturdy surface for the new tile, then lay out the tile pattern. Next, you mix up the adhesive and set the tiles in the layout grid, cutting them to shape as necessary. Along the way, you'll be making decisions about how to arrange the tiles so they look their best, and picking up a few specialized tools to cut and spread the materials.

While colorful tiles and fancy designs often get the most attention, it's a sound knowledge of the tilesetting basics covered in this chapter that will make your project a success. Later chapters will explain the special techniques used to tile floors, walls, and countertops.

Demolition

When you add tile to a room, you usually end up doing at least some demolition. Demolition doesn't take much skill – just the ability to do a lot of heavy work and to put up with dusty, messy conditions. If you're installing a tile floor, demolition may include pulling up old tile, vinyl, or wood flooring. Old ceramic tile can be a real chore to remove, since professional tilesetters often set tile on an inch or so of mortar (frequently reinforced with wire mesh). It's easiest to remove vinyl tiles if you use an iron or heat gun to soften the adhesive under the tiles before prying them up with a putty knife. When removing sheet flooring, you can set a circular saw to cut to the depth of the flooring plus the underlayment, then saw the whole thing into workable sections and pry up the flooring along with the underlayment.

Walls must also be properly prepared for new tile. Old tile can be removed from wall surfaces by breaking it up with a cold chisel and hammer, then pulling the pieces off with a pry bar. However, if stripping off old wallcovering or paint leaves large areas of white gypsum core exposed, the tile adhesive won't stick, and you'll need to install new drywall. For this reason, it's often faster and easier to remove the tile and drywall together, then install fresh underlayment for the new tile. Since demolishing walls always produces more waste than you think it will, you may want to spring for a small dumpster to hold the mess.

Protect yourself during demolition by wearing the proper safety gear. There'll be dust, debris, and noise, so wear eye and ear protection, heavy work gloves, and a dust respirator. Before cutting into walls and floors, make sure you know the location of any pipes and wires inside the wall, and shut off the water and electricity; test the wires with a current tester to be absolutely sure they're dead. If you remove a toilet during demolition, stuff a rag into the drain to prevent sewer gasses from entering the house and construction debris from falling into the drain and plugging the line.

The simplest way to take out old floor tile is to bust it up with a sledgehammer or maul. You'll want to remove both the tile and the layer of mortar that you'll typically find under professionally tiled floors. Be careful not to crack plaster walls (or the ceiling below) when busting up old floor tile.

Surfaces to be tiled must be clean, dry, and dust free. Strip off wallcovering and adhesive leftovers – as well as peeling paint – with a broad knife. If you'll be tiling directly over glossy paint, rough it up with coarse sandpaper before setting any tile.

Removing old ceramic tile from walls is fairly easy. Use a hammer to break through the surfaces. A pry bar will help you pull away the old tiles. If you're planning to replace the underlayment anyway, it's easiest to remove chunks of drywall and tile together.

Backer Board Basics

When laying out backer board panels, always line up the long edges of the panels next to each other. These edges are slightly tapered – the way they are on drywall – so the filled joints will be flush with the rest of the panel. In a typical tub alcove, a vertical 3x6 panel covers each end wall; the back wall is covered with two horizontal 3x5 panels. Position backer board with its textured side exposed if you'll be setting tiles in thinset adhesive. Face the smooth side out if you'll be using mastic. Leave about a ⅛-inch gap between backer board panels. The joints get filled with thinset adhesive and covered with fiberglass mesh tape.

Backer board is fastened to walls with screws or nails, but on floors it's embedded in thinset adhesive as well as being secured with fasteners. Whether attaching backer board with screws or nails, put a fastener every 6 or 8 inches around the edges and in the field. To keep the edges from crumbling, hold fasteners back about ½ inch from the edge. Both nail and screw heads should be set flush with the surface.

Always let the joints cure overnight before installing the tiles. Stay off backer board set on floors until the adhesive has cured. If you have to walk on it, at least stay off the joints between panels.

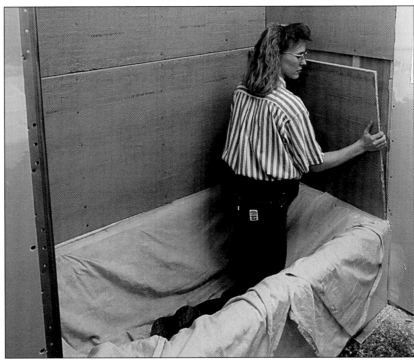

Install backer board with the panel edges centered on the wall studs. Backer board is sized so you usually can cover a tub surround without too many cuts.

Secure the backer board to the subfloor with 1¼-inch galvanized screws. Buy the type that are designed for backer board; they have a special head that grips into the backer board without breaking the mesh.

Lay out, cut, and dry-fit all the backer board panels before you secure them to the subfloor. Make sure to stagger the joints between backer board panels so they don't line up with the joints in the subfloor or with each other. Secure the panels to the subfloor with thinset, but be sure to finish the layout before you mix the thinset or it will become unworkable before you can use it.

If you prefer nails, use 1½-inch hot-dipped galvanized roofing nails. Nailing and screwing patterns are the same – every 6 to 8 inches around all panel edges and in the field.

Straight cuts

Cutting backer board is a lot like cutting drywall, except that backer board (because it's made from cement sandwiched between layers of fiberglass mesh) is much harder. The basic procedure for cutting backer board is to score the surface a couple of times, then snap the pieces apart along the score line. Use a carbide-tipped scoring knife designed for use with backer board panels. Or, you can cut backer board with a masonry blade in a circular saw or a diamond blade mounted in a power grinder. These methods leave a smoother edge, but the rough edge left by the carbide-tipped cutter isn't really a problem in most installations. Power saws also generate a lot of dust, so wear a dust respirator and work outside.

1 *Lay the panel flat* and score it with a carbide-tipped scoring knife. Hold the material firmly, and push down hard with the knife. Use a drywall T-square or straightedge to guide the cut.

2 *Break the board* with a good snap along the score line. It helps to slide the score mark to the edge of a table or workbench, then snap the panel down with a sharp motion.

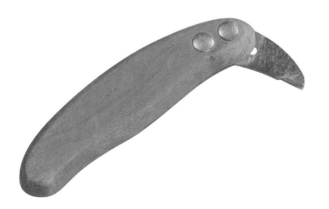

3 *The last step* is to cut through the fiberglass mesh backing with a sharp utility knife. It may be easier to stand the backer board panel on edge while doing this.

Cutting holes

Cutting holes in the backer board to accommodate fixtures, valves, and spouts isn't difficult, but it does require a different technique than cutting a straight line. First, draw the hole on both sides of the backer board panel. Then deeply score the cut on both sides of the panel with a carbide-tipped scoring knife; bear down hard to cut through the mesh. Finally, tap a hammer around the inside of the opening to break out the piece. Be gentle – you don't want the panel to shatter. You can also cut holes with a carbide-tipped hole saw.

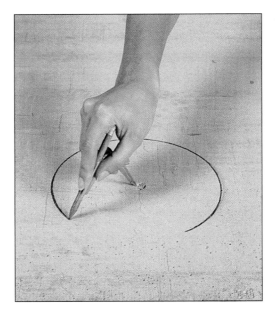

1 *Use a scribing* compass to trace the circle onto both sides of the backer board. To make sure the circles line up, first drive a nail through the center of the area to be cut out. Position the point of the compass in the nail hole.

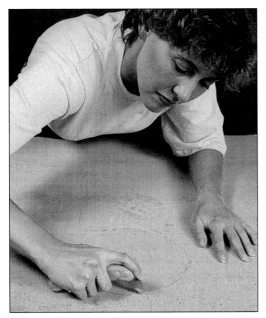

2 *Score the circle* on both sides of the panel with a carbide-tipped scorer. Make several passes to be sure the marks are deep.

3 *Several light blows* with a hammer should knock out the waste piece. Try to strike as close to the score marks as you can, supporting the underside of the backer board with your hand as you work.

Taping and mudding

Every joint between backer board panels must be filled with thinset adhesive, a process called mudding, then taped. Like drywall, the long edges of backer board sheets have tapered edges so you can fill the joints flush to the surface.

Start by filling each seam with thinset. (Use thinset to fill the joints, even if you'll be setting tiles with mastic.) Then lay a strip of mesh tape in the thinset and embed it with a broad knife. Always use the tape recommended by the backer board manufacturer to finish off the joints between panels; never substitute the fiberglass tape designed for use with drywall. Since your goal is a smooth, even surface for the tile, feather out the edges of the adhesive to get rid of any large ridges.

Use a broad knife to fill the joints with thinset. Don't worry about smoothing the mud, just make sure it's filling the gap between the panels.

Embed a piece of mesh tape in the thinset. As you pass over it with the broad knife, enough thinset should ooze up through the tape to cover it.

Layout Basics

Figuring out a tile layout can be one of the most confusing parts of a tile project. It usually involves quite a bit of juggling as well as a few trade-offs, but the following principles should help guide your decisions.

First, always follow the golden rule of layout, which says to set full tiles in the most visible areas of a room, and to hide cut tiles in less visible areas. Furthermore, cut tiles should be at least a half-tile wide, because skinny tiles are hard to cut, hard to set, and unattractive. Generally, it's best to choose the option that gives you the widest possible tile along either side of the installation.

Second, try to center the tile layout on the room's focal point, such as a fireplace or window. With floors, sometimes the doorway into the room will be the most visible spot in the layout. Not only do you want full tiles there, you want them to be centered on the doorway.

Third, if you will be tiling walls as well as the floor with tile of the same size, take time to consider how the floor layout will work with the wall layout. The project will look much better if the grout joints on the horizontal surfaces align with those on the vertical surfaces.

Some installations, such as out-of-square rooms, are harder than others to lay out. And some tile projects, no matter how much you try, will always have a design flaw. All you can

Straight and square reference lines *will help you figure out a tile layout that works for your space. Dry-lay tiles along the lines to double-check the layout, to see where tiles will have to be cut, and to determine what size they will have to be. Adjust the layout as necessary to vary the width of the cut tiles.*

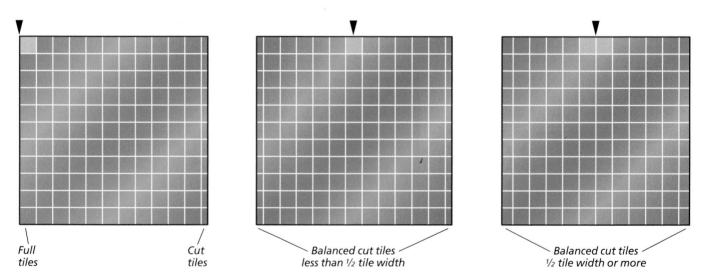

Full tiles

Cut tiles

Balanced cut tiles less than ½ tile width

Balanced cut tiles ½ tile width or more

Layout is a juggling act *– and you'll have to make some compromises. In this example, starting the layout with a full tile at one side of the room (left) results in one row of cut tiles at the other side, a situation you want to avoid. Centering the layout in the room (center) gives more balance, since the project will be capped at the ends with equal-sized cut tiles. Still, in this example, the cut tiles are narrower than the preferred half-tile width. Probably the best solution here is to shift the layout by one half-tile (right). This results in a balanced layout, with two symmetrical rows of cut tiles that are wider than the cut tiles in the previous example.*

do is to bury the flaw where it will be least visible, such as under a baseboard or cabinet or in an inconspicuous area of the room.

Reference lines

Some tilesetters rely on only a few reference lines, but we prefer to set up a grid of reference lines. On floors, start by snapping two perpendicular reference lines that run the length and width of the room. Test-fit a row of tiles along these lines to see how they'll lay out. You'll probably have to shift the lines to make rows of cut tiles come out even or to prevent a narrow row of cut tiles at the edge of the installation. After you develop the layout, you snap a grid of layout lines to guide

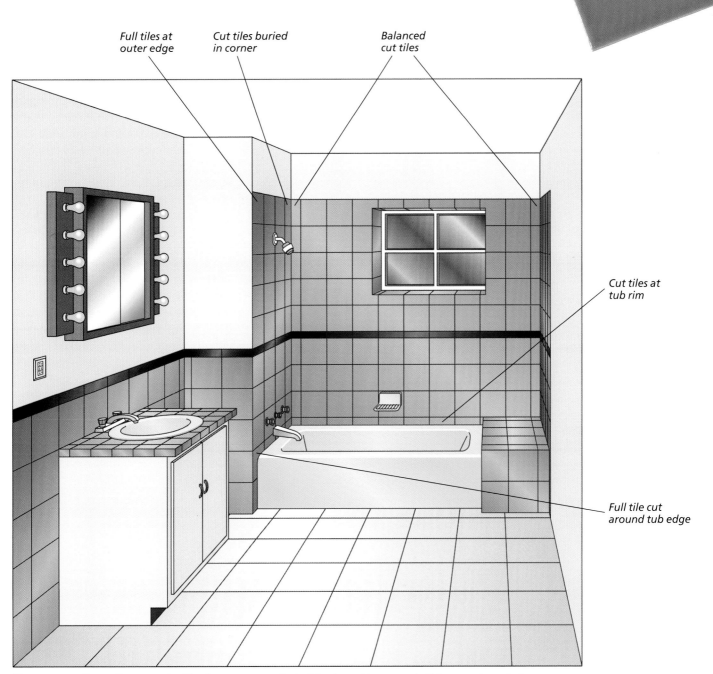

Full tiles at outer edge

Cut tiles buried in corner

Balanced cut tiles

Cut tiles at tub rim

Full tile cut around tub edge

The more surfaces there are to tile, the more complicated the layout becomes. In this example, note how the grout joints align from one wall to the next. In the tub surround there are equal-sized cut tiles at both edges of the back wall and full tiles along the exposed outer edges of the end walls. The row of thin cut tiles along the tub edge is less than desirable, but cutting them allows a row of full tiles where the wall meets the floor and a full tile that can be cut to fit around the tub's curved edge.

A story pole is useful for layout and for tilesetting. To make one, lay out up to 10 tiles with grout joint spaces, measure the total, and use the average for marking the story pole. A 6-foot 1x2 or other strong, straight piece of lumber makes a good story pole. Include spacing for any pattern or accent tiles you will be using. A spacing chart accomplishes the same purpose, but you'll need to transfer measurements from the chart to the tiling surface with a tape measure.

the placement of each section of tile. Generally, a section is sized to accommodate full tiles in an area about 3 to 4 feet square.

When you're setting tiles on more than one wall, you need to mark a level horizontal reference line around the whole space. This ensures that the horizontal grout joints will meet up at every corner. Never use a tub or counter or other object in the room as the basis for a reference line – it may not be level.

Layout aids

Because tiles are rigidly geometric, they must be evenly arranged and equally spaced to look good. There are several strategies to help you create – and maintain – a precise layout.

Probably two of the most useful aids are a story pole and a spacing chart. Both let you work faster and more accurately. Since both give you the cumulative width of tiles and grout joints for six to ten tiles, you'll be able to see in a flash what your spacing should be during layout – and check the spacing of your tiles once you start setting them. If your tiles are square you'll need one story pole. If they are rectangular, you can use either two story poles (one for width and one for length), or one, marking one edge for length and the other for width.

You also need accurate layout lines – and lots of them. Just remember that your tile project will only be as accurate as your layout lines. Of all the lines you will draw, your first two perpendicular reference lines may be the most important. If they are not perfectly perpendicular, the rest of the layout will be off. Small surfaces are easy to check with a framing square, but for larger surfaces (such as a floor) the 3-4-5 method is more accurate. For really large surfaces, you can size up the triangle proportionally using multiples of 3-4-5, such as 6-8-10 or 12-16-20.

The 3-4-5 method of establishing a right angle guarantees accuracy when marking perpendicular reference lines on a large surface. Snap a baseline and mark a point 3 feet along the line. Then mark a point that is 4 feet out from the baseline. With your tape, connect the two points. If it doesn't measure 5 feet, readjust the 4-foot point until it does. This will take some going back and forth between the two ends of the tape until you achieve a perfect 5-foot dimension. Once you're satisfied, snap the chalkline to create a second line that's perfectly perpendicular to the baseline.

Setting Basics

After spreading the adhesive with the straight edge of the trowel, comb it out with the notched edge. Hold the trowel at a consistent angle so the height of the ridges will be uniform. The pattern of the ridges isn't important, since the tile will push them down.

Generally, it's best to install tiles in one small section at a time so you can cover the area before the adhesive skins over. An area of about 3 feet square is typical, but you may want to start smaller until you catch on.

Use the trowel recommended by the adhesive manufacturer. As a general rule, select a trowel with ⅜-inch-deep notches for setting tiles measuring 12 inches square or larger. Smaller tiles are best set with trowels with smaller notches – ¼-inch-deep notches are about right. Unless it says something else on the adhesive container, use square-notched trowels when working with thinset adhesives, and V-notched trowels when working with mastics.

Applying the adhesive

Spread the adhesive in the section to be tiled with the flat edge of the trowel, holding it at about a 30-degree angle. The amount of adhesive you apply should at least equal the depth of the trowel's notches. Then comb the adhesive into ridges, holding the trowel at about a 45-degree angle. Comb in from the edges, adding more or taking some out of the center, until you've got consistently high ridges over the whole area. Make sure not to cover up the layout lines with adhesive, since you'll need to see these as you work.

Before you go very far, pry up a tile to check your adhesive and your spreading technique. Slip your margin trowel under a

Order, order

If your project calls for both tiled walls and floors, start with the walls. That way you won't accidentally mess up the freshly tiled floor or subject it to unnecessary wear and tear. If the wall tile is going to sit on top of the floor tiles, however, you have no choice but to do the floor first. In this case, just stay off it until it has set, then cover the new tile floor with cardboard when you tile the walls.

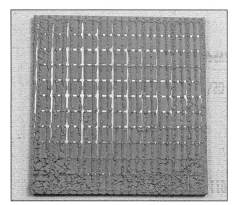

Less than full adhesive coverage on the back of the tile indicates that the adhesive was either too dry or you just didn't apply enough. If the adhesive is too dry, the ridges won't be evenly formed and you'll probably see gaps in them. For more coverage, try holding the trowel at a steeper angle or switch to a trowel with bigger notches.

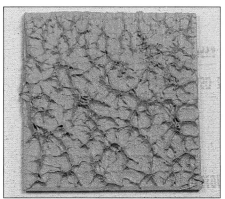

If the adhesive is glopped over the entire surface, you either made the mix too wet or put on too much. Overly wet adhesive won't hold ridges when combed. Unless you remix it, the bond won't be strong enough. For less coverage, use a trowel with smaller notches and/or hold it at a shallower angle.

The adhesive should completely cover the tile back. If it does, you know that the adhesive was mixed correctly (forming uniform ridges when combed) and applied thickly enough. When this is the case, about half the adhesive remains in the setting bed, while the other half clings to the tile back.

tile, twist it up, and evaluate the adhesive coverage. Don't set the test tile back after you're done checking. Instead, add a little more adhesive to the spot, comb it out, and set down a fresh tile.

Adjusting the amount of adhesive

Adjusting the angle of the trowel while combing will give you some control over the amount of adhesive you lay down. The larger the angle, the higher the ridges will be. Trowels with deeper notches will also create higher ridges. If the adhesive is the right consistency, but it's being pushed into the space for the grout joints, your setting bed is probably too thick. You'll need to reduce the angle of the trowel or use a trowel with smaller notches. In any case, make sure to keep the angle consistent to create a flat setting bed for the tile.

Setting tiles

At first, just concentrate on getting the tiles down. Don't obsess about alignment – when a section is done, you can fine-tune the spacing and make sure the tops of the tiles are flush with each other. Afterward, clean out any adhesive that has oozed up between tiles or been pushed out around the edges. If you leave adhesive in the joints, there won't be enough room for the grout.

For small cut tiles, you can trowel the adhesive on the underlayment the same way you would for full tiles. In tight places where a trowel can't reach, you'll probably have to

back-butter the tile with adhesive and press it into place. For a better bond, back-butter thick tiles with extra adhesive before you set them into the adhesive bed.

Maintaining the line

As you set your tiles, roughly align them to the layout lines. Keep consistent spacing between the tiles – it's critical for straight, uniform grout lines. Once a section is completed, spend a minute adjusting the spacing. Use your layout lines to make sure the alignment is perfect. If you made a story pole (p. 20) use it periodically during tilesetting to make sure that the tiles and grout joints are exactly where they should be.

Some tiles are cast with spacing lugs along the edges, so you can butt those up and get uniform grout lines. Most wall tiles have spacing lugs, but floor and trim tiles usually don't. Other tiles come pre-mounted on plastic or mesh sheets so that the spacing between tiles is already established and all you have to do is align the sheets.

Twist floor tiles slightly *as you set them in place. This helps spread out the adhesive under the tile, which ensures good contact between the tile and the setting bed. If the tiles are set closely together, you won't be able to twist them as you put them down, so just push each tile straight into the adhesive as firmly as you can.*

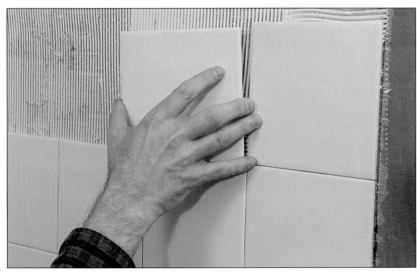

Set – don't slide – wall tiles *in place. Since most wall tiles have spacing lugs and are set close together, you won't be able to twist them without knocking adjacent tiles out of alignment. Just press each tile firmly into place.*

While you can buy plastic spacers to put between tiles, many tilesetters argue that spacers do more harm than good. For example, if the tiles vary at all in size, using a grid and eyeballing the grout joints allows you to make up size variations in the grout joints; using spacers in this situation would lead to an uneven layout. If you do use spacers, it's best to remove them once a section of tile is set. That's because with less grout over the spacers than in the rest of the joint, those areas tend to dry lighter in color. Also, spacers can cause the grout to shrink unevenly as it dries.

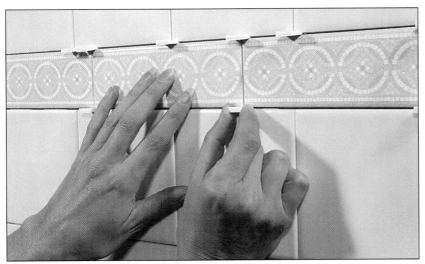

Use small wedges to space trim tiles and hold them in place until the adhesive cures. It isn't usually necessary to use wedges or spacers with regular wall tiles because most of them are made with spacer lugs molded in along the edges of the tiles.

Back-butter the tile with adhesive when there's no room to trowel the adhesive onto the underlayment, or when working with small tiles. Use a notched trowel or a margin trowel.

Set sheet-mounted tiles like large tiles, aligning the edge of the sheet along the layout lines. If there is any give to the backing (as with mesh), double-check that the tiles in the center of the sheet are straight after you set it.

Mark perimeter tiles in place after the full tiles have been installed. Position the tile to be cut on top of the last full tile and mark the overlap along the edges with a felt-tip marker. Remember to allow for a grout space and a ¼-inch expansion gap at the wall. The gap, which will be covered later, allows the floor and walls to move a little bit in relation to each other with changes in temperature and humidity.

Marking a notch cut is done in two steps. Place the tile on top of the tile that's nearest the corner and mark where it meets the wall. Then shift the tile to the adjacent wall. Hold it tightly against the edge of the previously installed tiles and mark where it meets the other wall. Lay a framing square on top of the tile and align it with the two marks. Draw lines to mark the notch.

Cutting Tiles

M ost tile projects involve at least some cutting. When two people are on the job, have one person cut tiles while the other person does the setting. On small projects, either make the cuts first or cut as you go; on large projects, cut as you go or do all the cuts last.

Marking

The key to accurate cuts – whether they're straight, curved, or angled – is accurate marking. Mark the faces since you cut the tiles face up. If your tiles have ridges on the back, it helps to mark the cut lines parallel to the ridges. This will make the cuts easier, neater, and more precise.

You can make straight cuts by transferring measurements to the tile to be cut, or you can set the tile in position and mark the cut line right on it. When you're measuring for your cut pieces, always remember to leave room for the grout joint. When marking perimeter tiles, you'll also need to leave room for a ¼-inch expansion gap along the walls.

Often you have to notch tiles to fit around outside corners. To do this you need to measure and mark for two cuts. To cut tiles to an irregular shape, around a door casing, for example, mark the outline with a contour gauge, then trace it on the tile. A simpler solution is to trim the casing to allow the tile to slide under.

Curved cuts are needed in bathrooms to fit tiles around the plumbing, but you also may need to cut tiles to trim out sinks and objects in other rooms. When marking a curve, it's easiest to set the adjacent tiles first, and then use those tiles to line up the tiles you need to mark.

To mark curved cuts around plumbing fixtures, pipes, sinks, or other objects, place the tile in position on the underlayment and draw the curve with a marker on the tile. Any rough edges of the cut will be hidden by the fixture escutcheons.

Straight cuts

Cut straight lines with a snap cutter or a tub saw. Snap cutters are available in sizes for large and small tiles, but some aren't long enough for 12-inch tiles (or smaller tiles that you turn in order to make diagonal cuts). Snap cutters are easy to use: First you score the tile, then snap it in two. If you've got lots of tiles to cut to the same size, renting a snap cutter with a fence will save you time. To avoid chipping out the glaze, always cut through the face of a tile, not the back.

Tub saws, also called wet saws, are worth renting if you have lots of tiles to cut. They're also essential if your tiles are too large, too thick, or too hard to cut with a snap cutter. Using a tub saw is also the neatest, most precise way to notch a tile to fit around a corner. But, because the saw blade is round, you'll probably have to turn your tiles over and finish the cuts from the opposite side.

To make a straight cut, position the tile on the tool bed and align the scoring wheel with your cut mark. Apply some pressure and draw the scoring wheel across the tile. Press down on the handle to snap the tile apart along the score line. Expect to waste some tiles; even perfect technique will result in a break now and then.

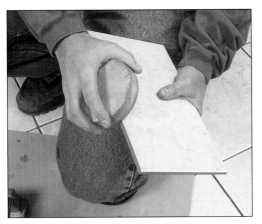

Smooth cut tile edges with a tile rub stone. If you don't have a rub stone, try substituting an abrasive stone or a piece of concrete.

Hold the tile in position on the plate of the tub saw and gently feed it into the blade to make the cut. Gloves and hearing and eye protection are a must when working with a tub saw. Since a tub saw will spray water, don't set one up in a finished part of the house.

Outside corners are easy to notch with a tub saw. Place the tile on the saw plate, orient one of the cut lines with the blade, and slide the plate into the blade, making sure you stop at the end of the line. Then rotate the tile and cut along the other line to complete the notch.

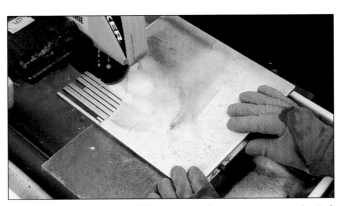

To make irregular cuts with a tub saw, first make a series of relief cuts in the tile, then break out all the small pieces with nippers. Work slowly and carefully to avoid ruining the tile. If you want the cut edge to be really smooth, you can dress it by running it across the blade of the tub saw.

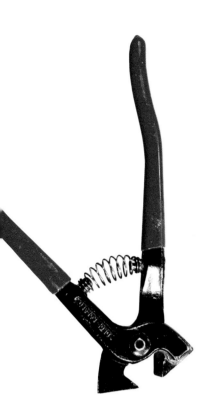

Curves and holes

The key to using tile nippers for curved cuts is to work slowly and to remove the waste in small bites, although you will still find that ragged cuts and ruined tiles are more the rule than the exception. Still, a ragged edge is no big deal since most plumbing fixtures have escutcheons that will hide any irregularity in the cut.

Rod saws cut curves and holes more slowly than tile nippers, but the edge is cleaner and the cut is more accurate. You hook the blade in a hacksaw frame or, to reach the middle of large tiles, into a coping-saw frame. If you have trouble finding rod saws at your home center, check the tile dealerships in your area. For perfect circle cuts, use a carbide-tipped hole saw bit with your electric drill. Start the hole saw in a pilot hole made by tapping the bit against the center point of the circle. When drilling holes in tile, always start at a low speed to prevent breakage, then run the drill at a faster speed as you go.

Cutting tiles with nippers takes patience – you have to nibble away at the waste in tiny bites until you get the right shape. Even when you're careful, you'll end up with a ragged edge. And it's really easy to break the tile, which means you'll have to start again with a new tile.

To cut holes with a rod saw, first drill a pilot hole, then thread the saw blade through the hole and attach it to the hacksaw or coping-saw frame. While you can hold the tile steady on the work surface with your hand, for complex curves you might want to hold the tile in a vise. Place the tile between two pieces of soft scrap wood to protect the tile face.

Drill a series of closely spaced small holes around the outline with a carbide-tipped masonry bit or a tile-cutting bit. Then tap out the scrap with a dowel smaller than the diameter of the hole. Be careful – you don't want the tile to crack.

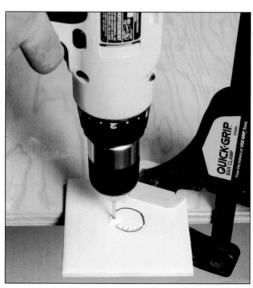

A spiral saw is an alternate way of slicing curves in wall tiles and other materials. It's also ideal for drilling holes. The cuts are clean and the saw doesn't need to be started in a pilot hole. Just plunge the carbide bit into the tile and begin the cut.

Installing a new ceramic tile floor *is a great way to liven up a room. Because there is probably no surface in your home that takes as much abuse as a floor, you'll need to pay extra careful attention to each step of the construction process. Rock-solid underlayment keeps tiles from moving or cracking. Adhesive that's been properly mixed and applied ensures a lasting bond. Grout that completely fills the joints between tiles keeps moisture from seeping underneath. It does take some time (about two or three weekends for 300 square feet of floor if you're working with a partner, more time if you're working alone), but the investment is well worth it.*

Laying Backer Board

In a complete kitchen or bathroom remodel it's typical to install new cabinets and countertops before putting in the floor. There are a couple of reasons for doing it this way. First, you won't mess up the new floor when you install the cabinets. Second, since you won't have to install tile under the cabinets, you can save a bit of money. On the other hand, if you tile before installing the cabinets, you won't have to cut and fit tile around them.

Remember, since tile floors tend to be a little higher than others, you have to make sure that the combined thickness of the underlayment and tile will work with adjacent floors, doors, and trim, as well as with the cabinets and undercounter appliances. You'll need to shim cabinets up to the height of the finished floor. Otherwise, you'll lose cabinet height when the toekicks get buried behind the tile, and undercounter appliances may not fit underneath the countertop.

Lay out, cut, and dry-fit all your backer board before gluing it in place. The alternative (cutting, fitting, mixing the adhesive, and fastening the panels all at the same time) requires high-speed action, and you will probably wind up with a bucket of hardening thinset. When dry-fitting the backer board, leave about ⅛ inch between the panels and hold the panels ¼ inch out from the walls to allow for expansion and contraction. Stagger the backer board joints and make sure they don't line up with the subfloor joints.

Mixing thinset

Thinset mortar is used for floors because it can support the weight that floors bear. Liquid latex and acrylic additives can be added to increase strength and flexibility (which can decrease cracking). You pour the powdered thinset into the additive and mix it in. If the thinset is polymer modified, it already has powdered additive mixed in, so all you add is water.

Properly mixed thinset looks like thick, stiff mud. A margin trowel makes a great hand-mixing tool, but you could also use a paddle chucked into a ½-inch drill.

Nail the backer board to the subfloor with 1½-inch galvanized roofing nails. Drive a fastener every 6 to 8 inches along the edges and in the field. Backer board screws hold better than nails, but they're also more expensive.

Prefill the joint between backer board panels using a broad knife, then set the fiberglass mesh tape over the joint. Make a second pass with the broad knife to smooth the joint and embed the tape in the mud.

Spread thinset evenly over the subfloor with the straight edge of a ¼-inch square-notched trowel, then comb it into ridges with the notched edge. Comb any excess into a pile and scoop it off. Add more thinset if the ridges are broken.

For most small projects, you can mix thinset by hand with a margin trowel. On big jobs you might want to rent a ½-inch electric drill and use a paddle bit to mix the thinset. Run the drill at slow speed and keep the paddle in the thinset – don't whip air into the mix.

Don't try to get all the lumps out right away. Instead, let the thinset sit, or slake, for about ten minutes after mixing. Slaking gives the moisture time to penetrate the lumps. Once the thinset has slaked, go back and stir it one more time to remove the last few lumps.

Attaching the backer board

When you spread the thinset, make sure to get good contact with the subfloor. Comb the thinset out with the notched edge of the trowel. Your combing job doesn't have to be pretty, just make sure the depth is consistent. Lay the backer board panel rough side up in the combed-out thinset. Do this right away or the thinset will skin over and the bond won't be as strong as it should be. Finally, fasten the backer board to the subfloor with nails or backer board screws. The pattern is the same for either fastener – every 6 to 8 inches along the edges and in the field.

Finishing the seams

Since they will be covered with tile, the joints between backer board panels will never be seen (unlike drywall seams) and they don't have to be sanded smooth. The seams must be level though, or the tiles won't be on the same plane when you set them. Force the thinset into the joints, lay down the fiberglass mesh tape, then embed the tape and level the joint with a broad knife. If you're applying sufficient pressure with the blade – and you've applied enough thinset – some thinset will push up through the mesh. When you're done, let everything cure for at least a day.

When to think about a mud job

Professional tilesetters often pour a ¾- to 1-inch-thick bed of reinforced mortar, or mud, as an underlayment for a tile floor. It's the best way to get an absolutely smooth, rock-solid, and crack-free tile floor. If your floor is badly warped, you might want to consider a mud bed to even out the floor. However, floating a mud bed is not a job for most D-I-Yers. Unless you are experienced, hire a professional to do this work.

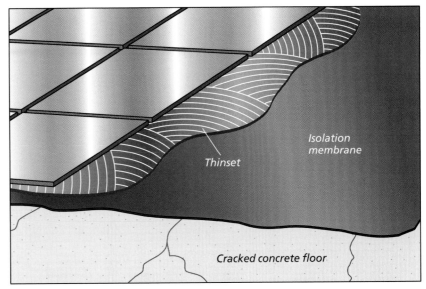

An isolation membrane is a thin, rubbery layer spread over the underlayment to isolate movement between the tile and the underlayment. It's especially useful when tiling over a cracked concrete slab because it keeps cracks from telegraphing through to the tile floor.

Isolation membrane comes as a liquid that is poured onto the underlayment or as a sheet material that is attached to the floor with thinset mortar.

Comb the liquid isolation membrane with a notched trowel to make sure the depth is even, then gently smooth over the ridges. Let the isolation membrane cure for about a day before tiling over it.

An expansion joint is a thin gap (about ¼ inch) that allows surfaces to move a little bit in relation to each other with changes in temperature and humidity without causing damage. In this photo the expansion joints have done their job – while the slab to the left of the joint has settled, no tile has cracked.

1 *Lay out one or two runs* of tile from the focal point into the center of the room, leaving space at the doorway for the threshold. Because they will be highly visible, the tiles in this doorway should be full tiles. Space the tiles in the layout using a tape measure and your spacing chart (or a story pole).

2 *Use a tape measure* and your spacing chart to see where the last full tile will be at the opposite wall. Then check the width of the cut tile you'll need to fill in between the full tile and the wall. In this case, the tile will need to be trimmed only slightly. To avoid trimming, you could try decreasing the width of the grout joints; this works sometimes, but not always.

4 *Lay tiles* from the chalk line out into other areas of the room. Use a tape measure and your spacing chart to figure out where the last full tile will be, then evaluate the width of the cut tiles: they should be no less than half, unless you're making a calculated trade-off.

Layout

There are two challenges in tile layout. The first is to figure out the arrangement of tiles that will look best in the room. The second is to mark some accurate reference lines so that when you set your tiles, they all line up.

Layout is fairly simple in a square room, but in rooms with openings to adjoining rooms or with lots of obstacles, such as

3 *Snap a second chalk line* across the room. Make sure this line is perpendicular to the first line, and that it lines up with the edge of a tile laid along the first line. If you're working alone, hold down one end of the line with a small nail.

kitchen peninsulas or island counters, things can get a little tricky.

In any room, the basic procedure begins with determining the focal point of the room. This is the one feature that draws your eye from the entryway – it may be a bathtub, a fireplace, a window, or a doorway. Try to center the tiles on that feature and to use only full tiles in that area. Snap a line perpendicular to the focal point and dry-lay a row or two of tiles to see where the last full tiles will fall and what size the cut tiles will be.

Now snap a line perpendicular to the first line. Position the line so it spans the entire room and is aligned to the edge of one of the dry-laid tiles. To make sure that the second layout line is perpendicular to the first, use a framing square or the 3-4-5 method of snapping right-angle lines (p. 30).

Dry-lay tiles along the length of this second line, checking the cuts at both ends to see if they're balanced in size. Adjust the first line back and forth as needed to balance the cuts at the ends of the second line. Remember, narrow tiles are hard to cut, hard to set, and they don't look good – beware of layouts that will require narrow cuts unless you can bury them under a cabinet or in an area where you'll have a lot of furniture. Dry-lay additional runs of tile to check where the cuts will fall against peninsulas, island counters, and other obstacles. Adjust the tiles as necessary until you have a pleasing layout.

Moving the tiles around on the lines can give conflicting results – you'll have to make some compromises. Adjust the lines until you've considered all the possibilities and have a layout you can live with. As you snap new lines, rub out the old ones to avoid confusion. If the walls of the room will be tiled, consider the impact the layout of the floor tiles will have on the wall tiles. If you're using tiles of the same size, try to line up the grout joints between floor and wall tiles.

Snapping grid lines

The more grid lines the better. These lines are your insurance against crooked, poorly spaced rows of tile and wavy grout joints. Use a framing square and a chalk line to mark a grid across the entire floor. Like your two major reference lines, the grid lines must be perfectly square to one another. Size the grid sections to contain full tiles plus their grout joints, but don't make the sections any bigger than 3 feet square – it's important that you be able to reach all sides of the section easily. Double-check the grid size by dry-laying tiles in one section.

Do the grid lines represent the center of a grout joint or the edge of a tile? The lines can represent either one, but be consistent throughout the project.

5 *Snap new chalk lines* as you adjust the layout. Be sure to mark out the old lines when you snap new ones.

6 *Divide the floor into a grid* once you're satisfied with the layout. Work carefully; the grid lines must be perfectly square. Size the grid so that each section is about 2 to 3 feet square and sized to contain full tiles plus grout joints.

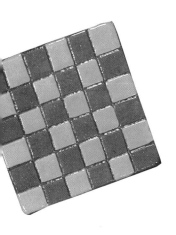

Quite a bit of juggling is required to balance the tile pattern in even a basic kitchen or bath. Figuring out the tile layout in a complicated kitchen or bathroom can try the patience of even a professional tilesetter. Shifting the pattern around to position cuts in the least visible areas is always a trade-off, since fixing a problem in one area often creates a problem in another area that was fine to begin with. You won't go wrong if you stick to laying out full tiles in the visible areas of the room, and tuck the cut tiles in less obvious places. In a complicated project, you might have to live with an area or two where the layout is less than perfect because the alternative may involve ruining the layout in a more visible part of the room. The illustration below shows some of the decisions and compromises we made when planning the layout for this kitchen.

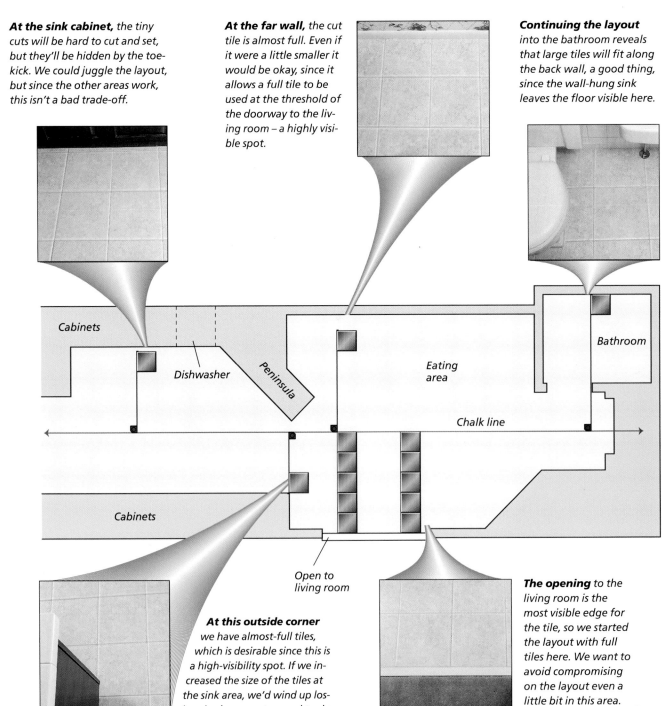

At the sink cabinet, *the tiny cuts will be hard to cut and set, but they'll be hidden by the toe-kick. We could juggle the layout, but since the other areas work, this isn't a bad trade-off.*

At the far wall, *the cut tile is almost full. Even if it were a little smaller it would be okay, since it allows a full tile to be used at the threshold of the doorway to the living room – a highly visible spot.*

Continuing the layout *into the bathroom reveals that large tiles will fit along the back wall, a good thing, since the wall-hung sink leaves the floor visible here.*

Cabinets

Dishwasher

Peninsula

Eating area

Chalk line

Bathroom

Cabinets

Open to living room

At this outside corner *we have almost-full tiles, which is desirable since this is a high-visibility spot. If we increased the size of the tiles at the sink area, we'd wind up losing size here – not a good trade.*

The opening *to the living room is the most visible edge for the tile, so we started the layout with full tiles here. We want to avoid compromising on the layout even a little bit in this area.*

Borders

A tile border adds color and detail to the room and can make any floor look like a custom job. But before you incorporate a border, make sure that the walls and floor in the room are fairly square and plumb. The straight lines of the tiles, especially if the border is a contrasting color, can really emphasize a room's irregularities.

The easiest border to install is one made of tiles the same size and style as the field tiles. This requires far less calculation and juggling than incorporating a border made of tiles that are smaller, larger, or differently shaped. Still, even when your border tiles seem the same in every way except color, make sure that the tiles are the same size; even tiles from the same manufacturer often vary a bit in size from color to color.

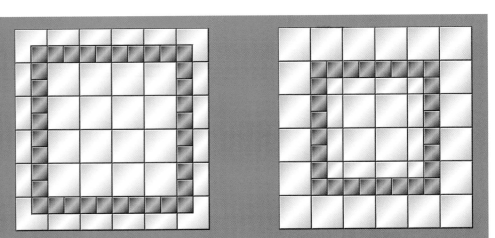

Careful planning is the secret *behind this intricate border and wainscot. Note how the diagonally cut tiles match perfectly where the floor meets the wall and how the full tiles are placed to continue the pattern from the wainscot onto the floor. A design this complicated must be carefully worked out on paper, then just as carefully transferred onto the floor and wall.*

Maintaining the line

When designing a border, you want the field-tile grout joints to continue on the same line once they cross the border. If your border tiles are a different size than the field tiles, you'll have to cut the field tiles just inside or just outside the border to keep the grout joints on track. Where you place the cut tiles affects the appearance of the floor, but only you can figure out what design works best for your situation. Be sure to consider both the size of the room and the size of the tiles.

When cut tiles are placed outside the border (left), *the eye is directed toward the border tiles and the full tiles inside the border. The notch-cut field tiles at the corners of the border look crisper than if you were to make the same shape out of a rectangle and a square. By contrast, using cut tiles inside the border (right) results in a much different look. First of all, the border is smaller. The design looks somewhat busy, and the eye is drawn outward to the full tiles outside the border as well as to the four full field tiles inside the border. It would probably work better in a larger space, with more full tiles inside the border. Where you plan your cuts is all a matter of personal taste.*

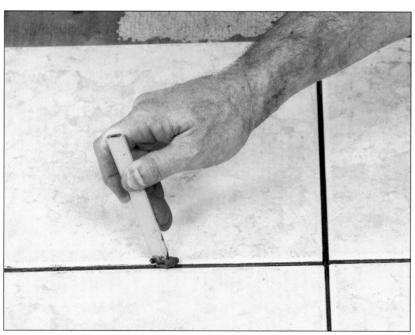

Setting Floor Tile

Floor tile is set with thinset mortar, the same material used to set the backer board. You spread it around with a trowel, making sure not to cover up your reference lines, then comb it into ridges.

Firmly press each tile into the thinset, then lightly twist it back and forth to ensure full contact between the tile and the adhesive. Don't slide the tiles into position. Work quickly, or the thinset will skin over and the tiles won't adhere properly. Once the tiles in each section are positioned, you can take a little time to fine-tune the spacing. When setting tiles, pry up a tile every now and then and check the back to make sure the adhesive coverage is what it should be (p. 31).

When working on a large floor, do all your cuts last. Let the full tiles set up before going back to set any cut tiles. When setting cut tiles, spread and comb thinset on the backer board; really small pieces in tight spots may need to be back-buttered. Always put the cut side toward the outside of the tiled area, so the uncut edges of the tiles are adjacent to one another. This will give you the neatest joint, since the cut outside edges will usually be covered up.

After floor tiles are set, you typically need to keep off them for at least one full day before you apply the grout. (Read the thinset manufacturer's directions – some products set up much faster.)

Begin setting tiles in a corner opposite an exit – you don't want to tile yourself into a corner. Work one small section of the grid at a time, laying the first tile in the corner of the section. Since the other tiles in the section key off this one, be careful to align the tile with both lines.

A little trim

Your project will look best if the flooring or threshold runs under the door jamb or casing. If it's necessary to trim a little off the bottom of the wood trim, do this with a handsaw or a jamb saw. Set the saw on top of a scrap piece of flooring or threshold material in order to gauge the height of the cut.

Scrape out any oozed-up thinset before moving on to the next section. If you allow adhesive to harden in the joints, you won't be able to grout the joints properly. Use a carpenter's pencil for wide joints and a utility knife for narrow joints. Keep a damp sponge handy to clean adhesive off the tile surfaces.

Thresholds

Where your tile meets another floor surface, you want a nice clean transition. There are several ways to do this, and the method you choose depends on the look you want, the material that the floor tile is meeting, and the height difference between floors. With any threshold, you need to plan for it during layout.

Thresholds come in wood, solid-surface material, metal, stone, and other materials. Some have a bevel on one side to ease the height difference between floors. Other thresholds have no bevels – they're just used to create a visual transition between flooring materials. Be sure to pick a threshold that will be flush with the top of the tile.

Wood thresholds make an attractive transition between a tile floor and a wood floor. If you're using tile for treads on a staircase, considering capping the front edge with pieces of metal threshold; tiled stair treads take a beating on the edge and will often crack or chip unless they're covered with metal threshold bars.

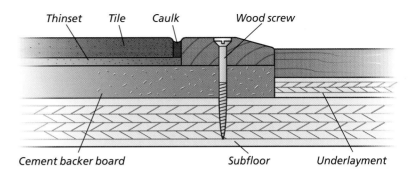

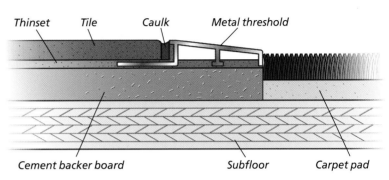

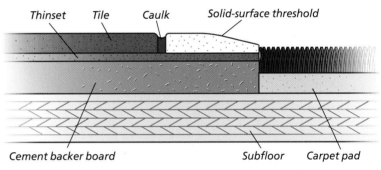

Wood and solid-surface thresholds go in place after the last tile is set (leave the width of a grout joint for caulk between). The bottom lip of a metal threshold goes in place under the last tile. The lip is perforated, and when you install it, the thinset squeezes up through the holes and locks the piece in place.

Back-butter a solid-surface threshold with thin-set, then set it in place, taking care that it's level with the tile. Leave space for caulk between the threshold and the tile. If you need to cut a solid-surface threshold to length, use a handsaw or a circular saw.

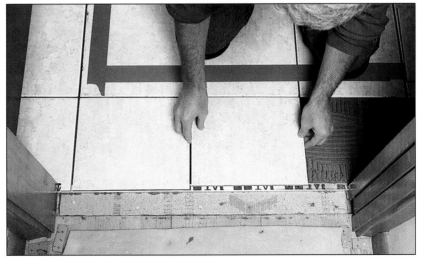

Embed an edge strip in thinset before setting the tiles over it. The edge strip protects the edges of the tiles and the adjoining carpet. It's a nice alternative when you don't want – or need – to install a threshold.

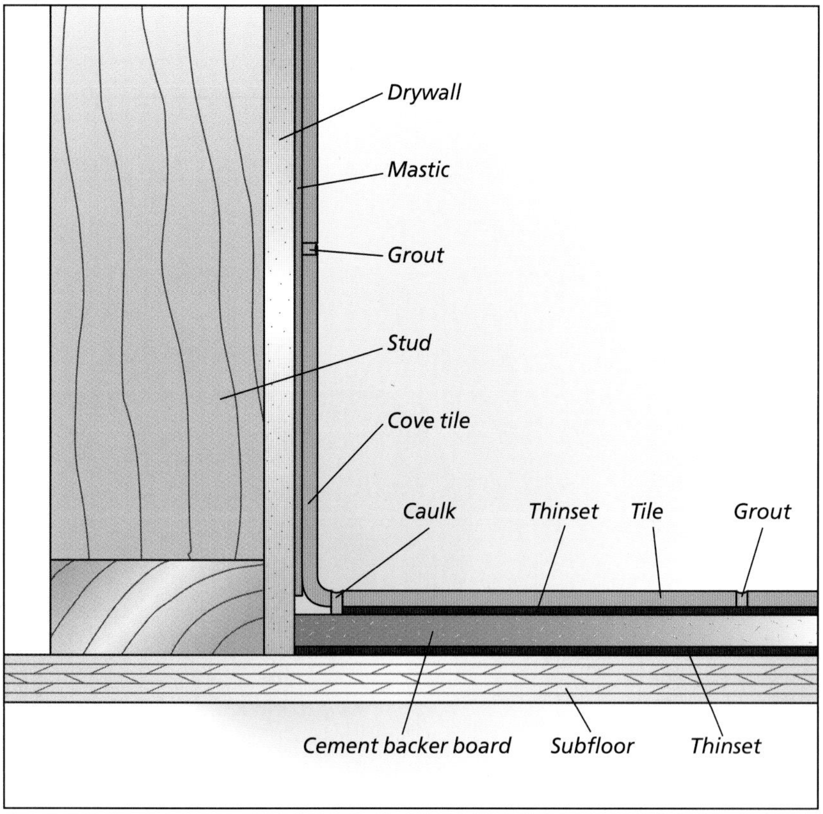

The diagram labels (top to bottom, left to right):

- Drywall
- Mastic
- Grout
- Stud
- Cove tile
- Caulk
- Thinset
- Tile
- Grout
- Cement backer board
- Subfloor
- Thinset

To keep cove tiles from cracking, *caulk the joint between the floor tiles and the cove tiles. Here, the gap under the cove tile serves as another expansion joint.*

Setting Base Tiles

Most tile manufacturers offer lines of trim tile designed to finish off the corners and edges of tile jobs. These tiles help give your project a professional look.

Base tiles are used in many tile installations in the same way that wooden baseboard is used to trim out a room. You can use either a single row of regular bullnose tiles or special base tiles. Some base tiles are flared at the bottom and make a clean transition from the wall to the floor. Use a base with a bullnose top if you won't be tiling the walls; choose a square-topped base if the walls will be tiled. Since it's easiest to put any type of base tile on top of the floor tile, you'll have to get your floor done before you put in your wall tile. Never cut sanitary base tiles for height; instead, cut the bottom row of wall tiles to make your layout work.

A cove tile has a concave curve that smoothes the transition from the floor tiles to the wall tiles. Coves can be installed anywhere two perpendicular surfaces intersect, and on any type of underlayment. You'll need to caulk – not grout – the joint between the cove tiles and the floor tiles or it will eventually crack. Like base tiles, cove tiles can be rounded on the top (to cap off the installation) or flat (when wall tiles will be set above the cove tiles).

When shopping for trim tiles you'll find that bullnose, cove, and other trim tiles are sold either by the lineal foot or by the piece.

These base tiles *sit on top of the floor to form a ceramic baseboard. Many types are available, including styles that turn corners. The tiles shown have rounded tops to cap off the project. Tiles that will be buried in an installation have flat edges to join up with wall and floor tiles.*

A row of buried cove tiles *creates a smooth transition from floor to wall. Besides looking good, this type of installation is easy to clean. The floor tiles are set first, then the cove tiles, and finally the wall tiles.*

Pieces of bullnose tile *can be used to form a tile baseboard. The joints between the bullnose tiles should be grouted to match the floor grout. Run a bead of caulk into the joint where the wall tile meets the floor tile.*

WALLS

Tiling a wall is an opportunity *to exercise your creativity. You'll get to select from a wide array of trim and accent pieces to customize your job. These pieces may be functional, such as soap dishes, grab bars, and towel hooks, or simply decorative. Either way, incorporating these special pieces doesn't have to be complicated, you just have to spend a little time during layout to make sure everything will work together. As with any tile project, expect to make some layout compromises for the sake of the overall look of the job.*

Install a vapor barrier over the insulation in tub and shower areas to protect the studs and insulation from humidity. Use as few staples as possible, because each hole lessens the efficiency of the vapor barrier.

Backer board must be installed on studs with edges that are all in the same plane, otherwise tiles and grout installed over the high spots are likely to crack or pop off. Use a 4-foot level to check that the stud edges are flush.

Underlayment

Cement backer board is an ideal underlayment for wet areas like shower walls and bathtub surrounds. Drywall, provided it's in good condition, makes a good underlayment for wall tile in dry areas. Don't just assume you can use moisture-resistant drywall, or greenboard, as an underlayment in an area where there will be direct contact with water because many building departments no longer approve it for that use.

Prep

Before you can install tile underlayment, you have to make sure all the studs are on the same plane. If they aren't, you have to plane down any studs that bow out, and/or fur out any low studs with builders felt or thin strips ripped from 2x lumber.

While the walls are open, you might want to beef up the framing to support a grab bar or pedestal sink. Cut 2x8 blocking to fit between studs and then nail it into place. If you aren't planning to make use of the blocking until sometime down the road, note the location of the blocking on your floor plan, or take a photograph of the wall before it's closed up. Back up either method by jotting down a few measurements as well.

Use a hammer stapler to staple felt furring strips to the edges of the wall studs to bring them all flush. The felt also protects the studs from moisture that may seep through the backer board.

Installing backer board

When used as an underlayment for walls, backer board can be attached directly to the studs. Where you'll be tiling one section of a wall and painting the other, you may find yourself joining the edge of a backer board panel to the edge of a drywall panel. Try to use backer board that is the same thickness as the drywall, or you will have to fur out the studs with strips of builder's felt to make the backer board flush. You should also think about the transition from the backer board to the drywall during tile layout. Since backer board doesn't take paint very well, the last row of tiles should overlap the drywall, not stop where the two materials meet.

Most tiles are attached to walls with mastic instead of thinset. This is because mastic has the ability to grip tiles even before it has fully cured, which prevents the tiles from creeping down the wall in the meantime. On walls that will have direct contact with water, professional tilesetters use thinset because it has greater moisture resistance than mastic. However, even pros will admit that it's much harder to set wall tiles with thinset than with mastic. To keep the tiles from slipping down the wall, they sometimes resort to taping the tiles in place or temporarily tacking a small nail under each tile to support it until the thinset cures.

The adhesive you use will influence how you install the backer board: smooth side out when the tiles will be set in mastic, rough side out with a thinset setting bed. However, the joints between the backer board panels will be filled with thinset, even if the tiles will be set with mastic.

Cover the bathtub – or any other fixture – with a blanket before you begin to protect it from chips or scratches.

Nail backer board to the studs using 1½-inch galvanized roofing nails, spaced every 8 inches. You can also use 1¼-inch or 1⅝-inch backer board screws – their threaded shanks grip better than nails and are less likely to pop out.

Backer board panels may be installed vertically or horizontally as long as the edges land on a stud. Because they come in a variety of sizes, backer board panels fit most tub and shower walls with a minimum of cutting.

A handy prop

Leave a ¼-inch gap between the backer board and the edge of the tub or shower pan to allow for a bead of caulk there. Nails set above the tub edge mark the gap and help hold the backer board in place while you're driving in the fasteners.

Leave a ⅛-inch gap between panels to allow for expansion and contraction. A nail makes a good spacer.

Apply a generous coat of thinset along the seams between panels, then lightly press a length of fiberglass mesh tape into each seam. Level the joints with a broad knife.

Tub Surround Layout

While the layout of tiles in a tub surround is not much different from the layout of tiles on other walls, there are a few extra considerations. The close spacing of the walls in a tub surround can magnify any imperfections, from tile rows that aren't perfectly level to grout joints that don't line up in the corners. No matter how eager you are to start laying tile, it's important that you take the time to draw some level and plumb working lines and to figure out how the tiles will look once they're on the walls.

Where to start

Begin your layout at the back wall of the tub surround. First draw a level horizontal line above the tub. Don't make the mistake of using the top edge of the tub as a reference point, since tubs are rarely level. Instead, find the low point of the tub with a level, put a ¼-inch spacer at that point (to allow room for caulk later), and then hold a tile on top of the spacer. Mark the top of the tile on the wall. This mark will guide you in drawing a level line across the wall. Expect to cut most of the tiles that fall below the line if the tub isn't level.

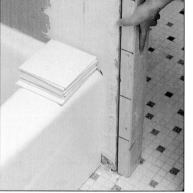

Check the layout in several spots to get a good look at your options. Here, starting the layout with a full tile above the tub edge would require a difficult cut in the tile that curves around the tub edge. Starting with a full tile at the floor instead will make the curve easier to cut and better looking, too.

Check the vertical layout of the tiles with a story pole. In a shower the tile should be installed to a height that's at least 6 inches above the showerhead. If you aren't tiling all the way up to the ceiling, draw a horizontal guideline to mark where the tile ends.

If the tub actually is level to within ⅛ inch, most professional tilesetters will draw the horizontal reference line measuring up from the highest point of the tub. This allows full tiles to be installed below the line. The little bit of deviation in the gap between the tub and the bottom of the tiles will be hardly noticeable once the gap is caulked. To make the first horizontal reference line, start at the high point of the tub, then measure up the wall the height of one tile plus the ¼-inch gap for caulking. Use a level to extend the horizontal reference line from that mark.

The vertical line

After you draw the horizontal line, draw a vertical layout line down the center of the wall. The entire layout will key off these two lines, so use a framing square to make sure that they are perpendicular.

Balancing the layout

The back wall of a tub surround will almost always look best if the tiles are centered on the wall. But remember the golden rule of layout: Cut tiles should never be narrower than a half-tile wide if you can avoid it. Therefore, when experimenting with your

Use a level to draw the layout line for the row of tiles along the edge of the tub. In this case, the line being drawn is based on the decision to use a full tile at the floor in order to simplify the cut of the curved tile at the edge of the tub. All the tiles below the line will have to be cut.

At the center of the wall, mark a vertical line that's absolutely perpendicular to the horizontal line. If these lines aren't square to one another, the whole layout will be off.

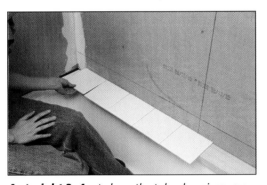

A straight 2x4 set along the tub edge gives you a place to set the tiles while you play with the layout. Start from the center of the wall and work out toward the edge. In this attempt, centering a tile on the vertical line yields a narrow piece of tile at the corner.

Shifting the layout one-half the tile width – in this case placing the grout joint on the vertical layout line – yields a tile of almost full width at the corner.

tiles, shoot for a layout that will result in the largest cut tiles at each edge of the wall. Small tile slivers are ugly to look at and hard to set – if you're winding up with them, try shifting the layout by half a tile. In other words, if you started out with a grout joint centered on the vertical line, shift the layout so that a tile is centered on the line instead. Use a piece of wood set on the edge of the tub to hold the tiles while you're playing with the tile layout.

On the end walls use full tiles at the room-side edge (the most visible part of the enclosure). This holds true even if it will result in a narrow cut at the inside corner where the end walls meet the back wall.

Use a level to extend the layout lines around corners. This will keep the tiles and the grout joints even as they wrap around the room. Here, only the shower walls will be tiled full height; the rest of the walls will have a tile wainscot so the layout line marks the top of the wainscot tile.

Laying out the end walls

Laying out the end walls is simply a matter of extending the existing horizontal reference line from the back wall onto the end walls. If you'll be tiling adjoining walls, you will also have to transfer the layout line to those walls. Work carefully because mistakes made now will be obvious after the tile is installed.

In rooms where a wall extends past the tub, you may not want to tile the whole wall. In this case, draw a vertical line to mark your ending point. The job will look best if you extend one row of bullnose or other trim tiles beyond the edge of the tub, running it from the floor to the height of the tile in the enclosure.

If you won't be tiling right up to the ceiling, draw horizontal lines on all the walls to mark where the tiles will end. This reminds you not to slop adhesive onto surfaces that will be painted. Use your story pole to determine where the last row of tile will be, mark the wall, and draw the line.

Marking accessories

As a last step, mark the location of any accessories, such as soap dishes or towel bars, that will be attached to the backer board. Since accessories will be installed after all the tile is set, be careful not to spread adhesive in these areas while you're tiling.

Lay out tiles on the end walls the same way you did on the back wall – with a piece of wood and a handful of tiles. Pay particular attention to the width of the tile at the outside (room) edge of a wall. Ideally, you want a full tile there even if it means using a narrow cut at the inside corner to accomplish it.

Use the horizontal layout line to mark the tiles for cutting. If the tub is out of level, each cut tile along the tub edge tile will be a slightly different size and will need to be marked individually.

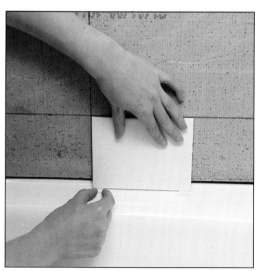

Leave a ¼-inch gap between the tile and the tub edge. Plastic tile spacers maintain the gap and hold the tile to the line. The gap will be filled later with caulk.

Setting Tub Surround Tile

It's important to use the right trowel for the adhesive you'll be working with. Unless the manufacturer says otherwise, use V-notched trowels with mastics, and square-notched trowels with thinsets. Whichever adhesive you use, don't spread adhesive in the area where a soap dish or other accessory will go, since these get set last.

Setting the back wall tiles

Start setting tile at the bottom of the back wall at the intersection of your reference lines, and work out toward the edges. Carefully align each tile and press it into the adhesive. If you find that your adhesive isn't gripping the tiles firmly enough to keep them in place, you can shim them with small plastic wedges, tack small nails under the tiles, or hold them in place with short strips of masking tape.

After setting the tile, quickly clean off any adhesive that squeezes up into the grout joints or onto the tile surfaces.

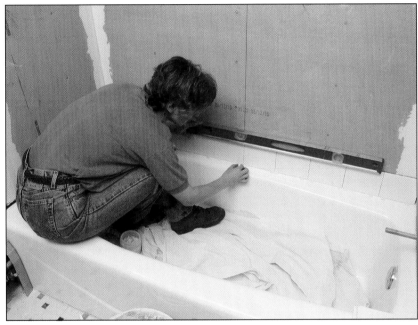

After setting the first row of tile, check the tile edges with a level or a straight-edge. This row will determine the position of the rows to follow, so you have to get it right. Use small wedges to shim the tiles up to the line.

Hold the trowel at about a 45-degree angle when combing the adhesive into ridges. The pattern of the ridges doesn't matter, but the height of the ridges does – it should be uniform to provide a level setting bed for the tiles.

Adjust the tiles along the layout lines to ensure the grout joints will be straight and continuous from one row of tiles to the next. You should have a little time to fine-tune the position of the tiles before the adhesive begins to cure.

Check it out

Every now and then pull off a tile to check the adhesive coverage. It should look like the adhesive on the back of this tile. Too much or too little adhesive will weaken the bond between the tile and the substrate.

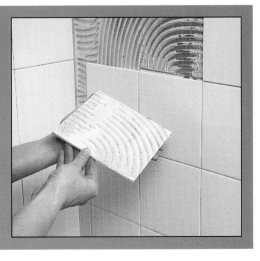

Setting end wall tiles

The plumbing stub-outs on a wet wall can make setting tile there a challenge. Unlike the rest of the job, wet walls will most likely require some curved cuts. While you may be tempted to make the cuts around pipes by splitting the tile in half and trimming a half-hole on the cut edge of each tile, don't. When you split a tile, the resulting joint isn't wide enough for grout or caulk, so it's easy for

water to seep in. Instead, use a hole cutter or a rod saw. And don't worry if the cut is a little rough, you won't be able to see it once the escutcheon plates are on.

Probably the toughest cut of all in a tub surround is a curved cut to fit the tile around the curved tub rim. What's really unfair is there's no escutcheon to hide a ragged cut here. If you can, use a rod saw or a wet saw (p. 35) to make this cut.

Hold the outside corner tile in place to mark the cut line. Remember to leave room for a bead of caulk between the edge of the tub and the tiles above it.

Expect to break a few tiles when you use tile nippers. To cut down on the breakage, take small bites and work slowly. A rod saw is a good alternative to tile nippers.

Check the fit before setting the cut tile. Remember to leave room for caulk between the tile and the edge of the tub.

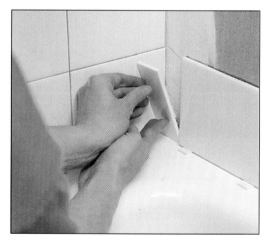

Set cut tiles with their cut edges facing into the corner. Leave a small gap for caulk between the corner tiles. Although this layout calls for narrow cut tiles, they'll hardly be visible in the corner and they allow a full tile at the room-edge of the wall – a good trade-off.

Setting trim tile

There's no better way to add a unique – and professional – look to your project than by incorporating trim tiles. They add flair to a job, and they're not hard to set. In fact, if you use trim tiles from the same line as your field tiles, you will probably find that setting them is no different from setting the field tiles. Trim tiles are even manufactured to wrap outside and inside corners. Unless they are set directly into the field tiles as an accent band or border, install trim tiles last.

There are two things to remember when setting trim tile. First, if the trim tiles are modular (meaning that one trim tile equals half a field tile or one or more full tiles), the grout joints of the trim pieces should align with the grout joints of the field tile. Second, do everything possible to avoid cutting trim tiles. For example, if you are using sanitary base tiles (tiles with a curved edge that bridge the transition from the wall to the floor) and they won't fit full size in your layout, cut the row of tiles directly above them, not the sanitary base tiles themselves.

Accent tiles are set the same way as field tiles because they almost always have spacing lugs built into their sides. But trim pieces, such as ropes and borders, usually don't have these lugs. Use wedges to space these tiles and to keep them in place until the adhesive cures.

When tiling around a showerhead it's important that the escutcheon plate rests completely on tile. You don't want it half on the tile and half on the wall because that could allow water to seep in around the showerhead.

The last tile on the outside corner of this shower installation has to cap off not only the top of the wall, but the edge of the wall, too. It's the perfect place to use a double-bullnose tile, which has rounded edges on adjacent sides.

Another double-bullnose tile caps off the square-edged field tile on the wet wall and makes a smooth transition to the wainscoting tile. Note that the wall tile above the tile being set is also bullnosed to finish off that edge.

Setting Accessories

Install toothbrush and cup holders, soap dishes, towel bars, and other ceramic accessories before you grout the tiles. The exception is any accessory you glue or screw on top of the tile. Attach these after the grout has cured.

Ceramic accessories usually have to stand up to hard use, so they need to be attached to the wall with a strong adhesive. Some professional tilesetters like to use regular thinset adhesive. Trowel the thinset both on the wall and on the back of the accessory, then set it into place on the wall. Silicone adhesive is also good for attaching accessories. It's easy to apply using a caulk gun. Some tile manufacturers make special fixture-mounting compounds formulated just for installing ceramic accessories. With this range of options available,

Press the accessory into position, *then secure it with strips of masking tape. After the adhesive dries – usually in about 24 hours – you can safely remove the tape.*

Apply silicone adhesive *to the back of soap dishes and other accessories. Run the adhesive completely around all edges of the accessory, then run a bead or two across the back.*

Use a combination *of hot-melt glue and silicone adhesive to set shelves and other accessories. The hot-melt glue helps anchor the fixture until the tile adhesive cures.*

there's no good reason to use mastic to fasten a ceramic accessory to the wall. The bond mastic provides is just not strong enough to withstand the wear and tear that most accessories endure.

You'll need to support the accessories with masking tape so they don't fall off the wall while the adhesive is curing. Use as much tape as necessary, pressing it firmly against the surrounding surfaces.

Support a shower shelf *with strips of masking tape until the adhesive sets up.*

To glue or not to glue

Some tilesetters claim that the best way to install a soap dish is to glue it to the underlayment. Other tilesetters believe that all soap dishes are destined to pop off the wall – no matter how they're installed – because people have a bad habit of leaning on them. They say that less damage will be done to the wall when the soap dish comes off if the soap dish is glued to the tile instead of the underlayment. We think your best bet is to avoid using the soap dish as a grab bar – or a few tiles may not be all you break.

COUNTERTOPS

Installing a ceramic tile countertop in a kitchen or bathroom is a little trickier than tiling a floor or wall. You'll have to work around sinks, ranges, cabinets, outlets, and switches – every one a special challenge to your layout skills. Still, a countertop project is well within the scope of a do-it-yourself project. Plan to spend a day doing demolition and installing the underlayment, a day or two setting tile, one day grouting, and another day to finish up with caulk and sealer.

If you'll be tiling both the backsplashes and the counters, do the countertops first. The joint between the two will look best if the backsplash tile rests on the countertop tile.

Underlayment

The material you lay under the tile needs to be selected with care. If the underlayment bends, expands, or contracts, the grout – and the tiles – will crack. While you could use two layers of ¾-inch exterior-grade plywood, we think that one layer of plywood topped with ½-inch backer board makes a stronger, more durable substrate.

Attaching the plywood to the counter

Cut the plywood to the overall depth of the counter, including the front overhang (a 1-inch overhang is standard). Since most cabinets are 24 inches, most counters wind up 25 inches deep. The tiles will generally add about another ⅜ inch to the front edge. Fasten the plywood to the cabinets with construction adhesive and screws. If the cabinets have corner blocks, drive screws up through the blocks into the plywood.

The bright white ceramic countertop and backsplash of this kitchen contrast beautifully with the deep color of the cabinets. Note how the backsplash reaches up to the bottom of the wall cabinets. Switchplates and outlets should be either on the backsplash or off it – never half on and half off.

Cut out the sink opening in the plywood before installing the backer board. Mark the opening, make some starter holes, then run a jigsaw along the lines and cut the piece out. A second pair of hands will keep the cut piece from falling out abruptly and binding the saw or splintering.

Mark the backer board for the sink using the cut plywood as a template. Place the backer board on top of the plywood then, from underneath, trace the opening of the sink through the cut onto the underside of the backer board panel.

Installing the backer board

The tricky part of installing backer board for countertops is cutting the openings for the sink and in-counter appliances, such as cooktops. That's because you can't use the score and snap method used for straight cuts. Instead, the opening must be scored onto both sides of the panel so the waste piece can be knocked out. To do this, cut the opening in the plywood first, then position the backer board over the plywood and trace the opening in the plywood onto the bottom of the backer board. Measure the exact location of the marks on the backer board so you can locate and mark the opening on the other side of the backer board. To cut the opening, score along the marks on both sides of the backer board, then tap out the scrap piece with a hammer.

Bond the backer board to the plywood with thinset. Set the panels rough side up, since countertop tiles are set with thinset adhesive. Space the panels about ⅛ inch apart.

Transfer the measurements of the cutout to the other side of the backer board panel. (When cutting holes in backer board you have to score both sides of the panel to make the cut.)

Once the backer board is in position, nail or screw it to the plywood every 8 inches around the edges and in the field. Nail and screw heads should be flush with – not below – the surface. Mud and tape the joints, then let the thinset cure for a day (unless you're using a fast-setting product) before you set the tile.

Backsplashes

When installing a ceramic tile backsplash, it's fine to tile directly over the existing drywall if it's clean and in good condition. If the drywall is damaged, cut out and replace the damaged section before tiling the backsplash.

Bathroom and kitchen sinks

When choosing a new sink, pay attention to the way the sink mounts to the countertop – it will affect how you tile around the sink opening and when you install the sink. Self-rimming sinks (the sink rim is supported by the counter) are installed after the tile is set and grouted. They're easy to install and are a popular option. Tile-in sinks are another good option. The square corners and flat edges of these sinks lay right into the tiled countertop. Choose an undermount sink only if your tile has trim pieces available to cover the edges of the underlayment around the sink opening.

Score the outline of the sink opening on the first side of the backer board using a carbide-tipped scoring tool. Then flip the panel over and score the panel on the other side. Gently tap around the inside of the cutout to knock out the waste. Go slowly so you don't shatter the backer board.

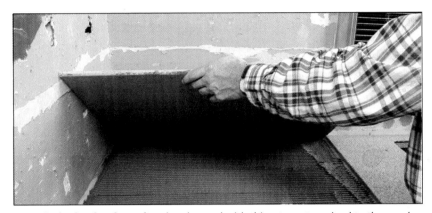

Attach the backer board to the plywood with thinset mortar mixed to the consistency of thick mud. To prevent the thinset from drying out before you can use it, do all your layout, cutting, and dry-fitting before mixing it up. After setting the panels in the thinset, fasten them with nails or backer board screws.

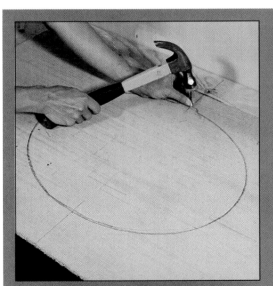

Drive nails around the perimeter of the cutout, spacing them evenly. Pull them out, then score along the outline with a carbide-tipped scoring knife.

Flip the backer board over and use the nail holes to align the template. Trace around the template, score the second side, then tap out the waste.

Other ways to locate sink openings

To make sure the score marks on both sides of the backer board will line up, you need to be extra careful when marking the sink opening. Nail holes make good markers when transferring the layout from one side to the other. Cardboard or paper templates are also useful. If you'll be reusing the existing sink, you already have a template – just use the dimensions of the opening in the old countertop to mark the new underlayment.

Layout

When laying out a countertop, there's really only one rule to remember: The front edge of the counter is the most visible part – make sure the layout looks good there. Follow this rule, and the rest of the layout will mostly take care of itself.

Do a dry run to work out the layout. Test-fit the edge tiles, then lay tiles from front to back to judge the size of the cuts. Next, fill in some field tiles so you can check how the cut tiles will fall around the sink – try to avoid slivers of tile there. You also want to check how the tiles fall at the countertop ends. When you're satisfied with the layout, mark reference lines on the backer board with a framing square and chalk line. Out-of-square counters (like out-of-square floors) may never look perfect, but there's not much you can do about it except run a row of tapered tiles along the back edge.

Laying out a backsplash

If you're using the same tile for the backsplash as you are for the counter, you'll want to continue the grout lines for the counter up the wall. Therefore, half of the backsplash layout – the side-to-side part – is already determined by the layout of the counter. The other half of the layout – the up-and-down part – depends on how high up the wall you want to run your tiles.

If you're not using the same tile, arrange the backsplash tiles so they complement the counter tiles.

The focal point of a straight counter is the row of full tiles behind the edge tiles. When doing this type of layout, first lay out the edge tiles then lay out the tiles front to back. Finally, adjust the field tiles as needed for balanced cuts at the countertop ends.

When an outside corner is the focal point on the countertop, start the layout there. Outside corner edge pieces are often available – all other tiles work out from that piece.

With an L-shaped counter, the inside corner is most visible, so snap lines behind the edge tiles and set a full tile at the intersection. The rest of the layout will key off this tile. If an inside corner edge piece is not available, miter the edge tiles that meet in the corner.

If your counter has two focal points, you'll probably have to make some compromises in your layout. Sheer luck created the almost perfect layout shown here: Starting with a full tile at the inside corner yields an almost full tile at the outside corner.

Another way to trim an edge

If your tile manufacturer doesn't produce edge trim pieces for countertop edging, bullnose tiles will work just fine. Use single bullnose tiles to edge the straight parts of the counter and double bullnose tiles for outside corners.

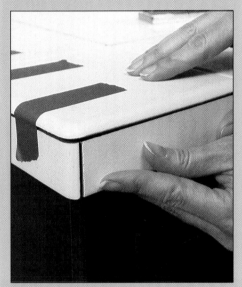

This edge treatment looks best when the edges of the bullnose tiles end flush with the faces of the front edge tiles, so allow space for adhesive behind the front edge tiles when planning the layout. A length of bullnose tile turned sideways eases an outside corner. Make sure the cut edges of the tiles face up.

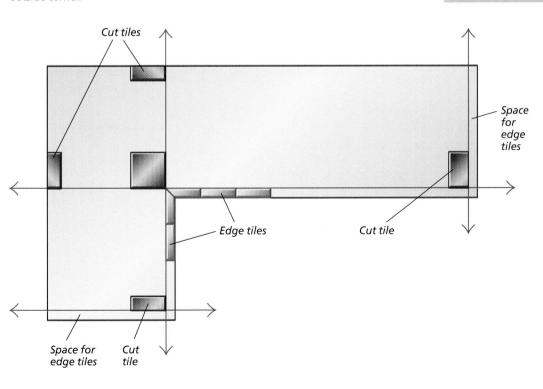

Cut tiles

Space for edge tiles

Edge tiles

Cut tile

Space for edge tiles

Cut tile

All tile layouts require some compromise and this example is no exception. A symmetrical layout will help the cut tiles blend in with the rest of the counter: Try to keep a full tile at the inside corner – it will look better than a cut tile and will be the key to the rest of the layout.

If the cut edge of the tile that goes around the corner of the sink edge looks ragged, it's really not much of a problem. The flange on a self-rimming sink will eventually hide the cuts. Use a rod saw, tile nippers, or a spiral saw to make curved cuts like this one.

Setting

Use thinset mortar to set countertop tiles. Spread it out in an even layer with the flat edge of the trowel, then comb it into even ridges with the notched edge. When you lay the tile, it will flatten out the ridges into a smooth, even setting bed. Remember to stay clear of the layout lines when spreading thinset.

Set each field tile by pressing it into the thinset adhesive with a slight twisting motion. This flattens out the thinset into an even layer, ensuring a strong bond between the tile and the backer board. As you work, pry up an occasional tile and check its back to make sure that you're getting good adhesive coverage (p. 31).

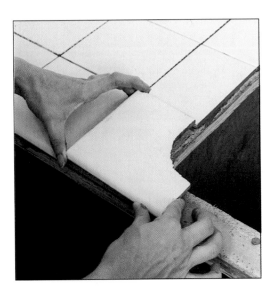

Whether you set the edge tiles first or last is a matter of personal preference. Setting them first provides a reference for setting the field tiles. However, you'll have to be careful not to dislodge them as you reach to set tiles along the back edge of the counter.

Once you begin to set the tiles, just concentrate on getting them down – don't worry

Lay the bullnose tiles along the edge. Every now and then, hold a cut tile under the bullnose to make sure that the bullnose overhangs it by the right distance. The joint between the bullnose and the cut edge tile should be perfect, even if it results in a little variation in the joint between the back of the bullnose and the counter tile behind it.

Some complex layouts call for fancy cuts. When positioning small cut tiles, either spread the thinset directly on the back of the tile or onto the countertop underlayment – whichever seems easiest to you. A margin trowel is helpful for getting into tight spaces.

too much about perfect spacing. Once a section is done, you can go back and eyeball the job, making any adjustments necessary to achieve consistent spacing and straight grout joints between rows. Quickly clean up any thinset that squeezes up between the tiles or gets pushed out at the edges.

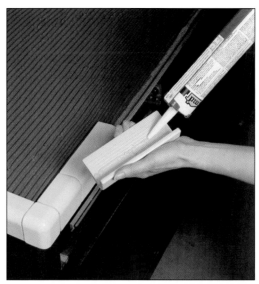

A combination of thinset and silicone adhesive holds V-cap edge tiles in place. Apply silicone adhesive behind the front edge of the tile; thinset holds the top edge.

Protect finished surfaces with masking tape before you start tiling. Narrow cut tiles are usually to be avoided, but here they allow a full tile at an outside corner – a good compromise in the layout.

Use silicone adhesive to attach the cut tiles to the front edge of the counter after the bullnose tiles have set up overnight. To keep the cut tiles from sliding down, tape them in place with masking tape.

Wood Edges

In addition to edge tiles and bullnose trims, wood edging is a popular choice for counters. Since it will have to withstand a great deal of moisture, make sure to seal the wood with a water-resistant finish on all sides before installing it. Set wood edging at a height that will be even with the top of the installed tile. Use tiles to help gauge the correct height, but don't forget to allow for the thinset under the tile. Use caulk instead of grout in the joint between the edging and the tile; a grout joint will inevitably crack since the wood and the tile expand and contract at different rates.

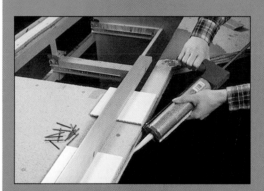

Attach wood edging to a countertop with construction adhesive and finishing nails. Predrill the nail holes before pounding the nails into the plywood part of the underlayment. Where the edging turns a corner, miter the two pieces of wood.

Leave a ⅛-inch gap between the wood and the tile. To eliminate cracking, fill the gap with caulk instead of grout.

Spread the mastic with the straight edge of the trowel, then comb it into even ridges with the notched edge. Work carefully around outlets, making sure not to slop mastic inside them.

Cutting a tile to fit around a windowsill is a challenge. If you're sure of your skills, you can make this cut with a wet saw. Make a series of cuts into the middle of the tile (p. 35), break out the pieces with tile nippers, then run the piece side-to-side against the saw blade to smooth the cut edges.

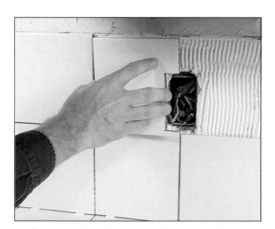

To fit around outlets, tiles often have to be notched. For the cleanest cuts, cut the notch on a tub saw. If the opening falls entirely within one tile, cut the opening with a rod saw (p. 36).

Backsplashes

Backsplashes can be as simple as a row or two of tiles run along the wall or they can cover the entire space from the countertop to the bottom of the upper cabinets. Either layout is fine, but the higher the backsplash, the more cutting you will have to do around outlets, switchplates, and windowsills. As a general rule, a backsplash should either stop short of the switchplates and outlets or extend past them; outlets and switchplates should never be half on and half off the tile.

Use mastic for backsplash tiles and, unless the manufacturer specifies otherwise, use a V-notched trowel to spread it.

As you set the first row, use tile spacers to leave a gap for caulk between the counter and the backsplash. If the tiles don't have built-in spacing lugs, wedges will keep the tiles from sliding down the wall while the mastic sets up.

Electrical boxes

When you set tiles around an electrical box, make sure the tile extends all the way to the edge of the box. Otherwise, the cut edges of the tiles may show around the outside of the coverplate. Also, pay special attention to boxes with GFCI receptacles, or with decorator-style switches and outlets. Since the cover plates for these attach outside the perimeter of the box, you'll need to notch the tile so that the screws don't have to be driven into the tile, which could break it.

GROUTING

One of the last steps in a ceramic tile installation is grouting the tiles. Working the grout across the tiles and packing it into the joints is hard work, but very rewarding. Grout is the element that pulls a tile job together, so this is when you finally get to see what it's all going to look like.

When you're picking out your grout color, remember that grout that blends in with the tile color will minimize the grout joints, while contrasting grout will accentuate them. If your project is a floor, stay away from white grout. It looks great at first, but it's very difficult to keep it from staining.

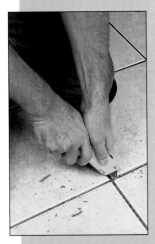

Before you start spreading grout, do a final check of the area to make sure that there isn't any mortar clogging up the joints. It's best to clean out the joints when you set the tiles, but it's easy to miss a few joints. If so, dig them out now with a utility knife. Vacuum out all debris before you apply any grout.

Mix the grout so it's fairly dry and stiff – it needs to be just workable enough to push into the joints. The drier the grout, the easier it will be to clean off the surface of the tile. After mixing, let the grout slake for about ten minutes so the moisture can penetrate the lumps, then gently mix the grout once more to dissolve any remaining lumps.

Preparation

You can begin grouting about 24 hours after setting the tile. Before you start, mask off any woodwork or carpeting so the grout won't stain it. Remove dried mortar from tile faces and make sure the joints between tiles are free of debris. Scratch out any adhesive that is high in the grout joints.

Use sanded grout for joints wider than ⅛ inch; plain grout for narrower joints. You can mix either type with additive to improve

Vacuum thoroughly before you start mixing and spreading grout. You need to get all dirt, dust, and debris out of the joints.

water-resistance and make the grout stronger and more flexible – and less likely to crack. You should use an additive anytime you're grouting an exterior surface or one that will have direct contact with water, such as a countertop or bathroom floor.

You can use a liquid additive instead of water to mix grout. Check the directions on the grout bag before using an additive; many manufacturers now add dry polymers to their grout mixes. If your grout is polymer-fortified, mix the grout with plain water.

A drill and mixing paddle can save a lot of wear and tear on your arm. This is the way to go if you will be mixing large amounts of grout. When you're mixing, don't lift the paddle up and down or air will get whipped in, resulting in a weaker grout.

Spreading Grout

Try to get all your grouting done in one day. If you do the work over two or more days, you may be able to see where you stopped and started again. Work in small sections – areas measuring about 4 feet square are about right.

Grouting is more monotonous than it is difficult. Just scoop the grout out of the bucket and onto the surface, then pack it into the joints with a rubber float, making several passes. Work diagonally across the tiles and angle the float about 30 degrees (this will help push the material between the tiles and eliminate air bubbles). Scrape off excess grout with the float held almost perpendicular to the surface, again working diagonally.

When you grout porous tiles like slate, marble, or terra cotta, the grout can penetrate the tile, leaving a dull, foggy appearance. To prevent this, seal the tile before you grout it, using the product recommended by the tile manufacturer.

Force grout into the joints between tiles with a grout float held at about a 30-degree angle. Make several passes in different directions to really work the grout into the joints. Because the float has a padded bottom, you can lean on it pretty hard without hurting the tile.

Hold the float on edge and scrape off the excess grout. Work the float diagonally across the tile so you don't gouge out the grout with the edge of the float. The grout should be level with the surface of the tiles.

Working in tight spots can be tough on your arm, but the procedure is no different from any other area. If you like, you can use a smaller float. Here, we've taped off the cabinets so the grout doesn't stain them.

Grout or caulk?

There are a few spots where grout will inevitably crack, so you'll want to use caulk there instead. Caulk provides a flexible seal between materials that expand and contract at different rates. You use caulk anywhere tile meets another material and anywhere two planes of tile meet.

Typically, you'll use caulk between floor tile and a cabinet toekick and at the inside corner where two walls meet. Other places to caulk are the joint between floor and wall tiles, around a toilet, between a countertop and backsplash, and around a bathtub or shower pan.

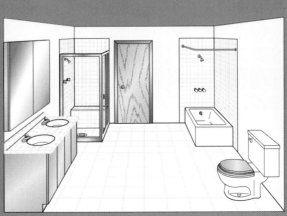

Cleaning the Tiles

After grouting an area of tile, wait for the grout to firm up slightly, then wash off the tiles. This usually takes about 10 minutes, but the time can be longer or shorter depending on the type of grout and tile, as well as temperature and humidity. For cleanup, you'll need a clean sponge and a bucket of cool water. Use a grout sponge – its rounded edges are less likely to pull grout from the joints during cleaning than the square edges of a regular sponge. The rounded edges are also handy for smoothing out the joints. If you find that your cleanup efforts are disturbing the grout in the joints, give the grout a few more minutes to set up. But don't wait too long or it'll be almost impossible to remove the grout from the surface of the tiles.

When cleaning off the tiles, it's important to use as little water as possible, since the grout will absorb excess water and be weakened by it. Cleaning happens in several stages. First you remove the bulk of the excess grout and shape the joints. Then you

1 *Wipe as much grout as possible off the surface of the tile. Use a clean sponge and make circular strokes in a slow, steady motion. Rinse the sponge often.*

Don't drink the water

Don't dump dirty grout rinse water down the drain – the solids can settle in the trap and drain-line. Instead, let the rinse water sit for about 15 minutes, pour off the liquid, then scoop out the solids and throw them away in the trash. It's safe to dump small quantities of rinse water (under 5 gallons) on the lawn – just make sure the water won't flow to a storm drain or waterway.

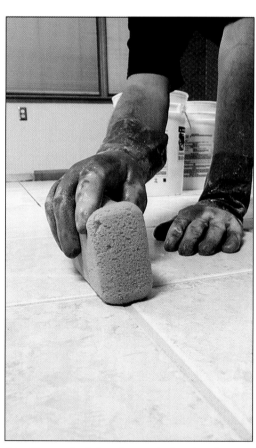

2 *Shape the joints by gently drawing the rounded edge of a damp grout sponge along the joints. The grout in the joint should be slightly below the tile.*

clear off the remaining grout, rinsing the sponge after each cleaning stroke. During this stage, always rinse the sponge after each pass. If you don't, the surface may initially look just as clean as the one you created with a freshly rinsed sponge, but once the tile dries you'll see more haze left behind.

Once you've finished cleaning off one area of tile, move on and start grouting an adjoining area.

Polish off the haze

No matter how well you rinse the tiles, when they dry off there will inevitably be a thin haze of grout left on the surface. This haze should be polished off quickly, since the longer you let it sit, the more difficult it will be to remove. On the other hand, make sure you wait long enough for the joints to set up a bit so you won't damage them when rubbing off the haze.

If you get delayed and the haze hardens, you will usually be able to get it off by scrubbing the surface with a white plastic scouring pad and plain water. Stubborn spots can be removed with a solution of white vinegar and water, undiluted white vinegar, or a chemical grout haze remover. However, these substances must be used carefully, because they can actually damage the grout in the joints while they're removing the haze on the surface. Your safest bet is to contact the grout manufacturer for recommendations on cleaning procedures and products for removing stubborn hazes.

3 *Make a final* cleaning pass across the tile. Use light pressure here – you don't want to disturb the grout joints at this point. Make only one pass with each side of the sponge before you rinse it.

4 *Rinse the sponge* clean and wring it out well after every single stroke. In the end, this continual rinsing will provide a much cleaner surface.

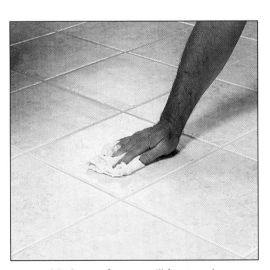

5 *A thin haze of grout* will form on the surface as the tile dries and the moisture evaporates. Polish off the haze with a clean, soft, lint-free cloth, like cheesecloth.

6 *If the haze hardens* before you get around to buffing it off, you can usually scrub it off with plain water and a white plastic scouring pad. If the haze is really stubborn, switch to a solution of vinegar and water.

Caulk and Sealer

Let the grout cure a couple days before caulking. While you can use a clear tub/shower caulk, try to get one that matches the color of the grout. Fill the joints completely, then smooth them with a damp rag or with your finger.

Sealing the grout joints makes them more resistant to water and mildew, and helps keep dirt out of them. When you seal the grout depends on the type of sealer you're applying. Some manufacturers tell you to wait a couple of weeks before applying a sealer so the grout will have a chance to cure thoroughly; other products can be applied as soon as 48 hours after grouting.

There are solvent-based and water-based sealers available. Some sealers will change the color of the grout slightly, others will not. Some need to be reapplied every 6 to 12 months, others last 5, 10, or even 15 years. And, of course, prices vary widely. To make sure you're getting the best sealer for your particular project, read the product specifications and directions carefully.

If your tile is glazed and some sealer dribbles onto it, just wipe off the sealer before it dries – it won't do any harm. If sealer does dry on the tile, try scouring it off with a white plastic scouring pad. If that doesn't work, contact the manufacturer for additional instructions.

We prefer to use a bristle brush, not a foam brush, to apply the sealer. Some sealers melt foam brushes and rough, sanded grouts can shred them, leaving pieces of foam trapped in the sealer.

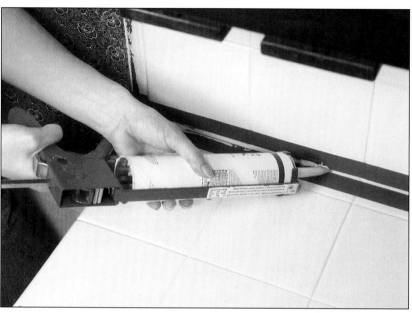

For an even bead of caulk, tape off the top and bottom of the joint and then run the caulk in between. The tape also prevents the caulk from creeping into the grout joints.

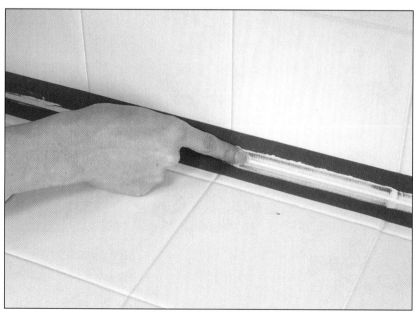

Smooth the caulk carefully with your finger. The excess will smear right onto the tape, which will be stripped off as soon as you're done smoothing. Keep a damp paper towel or rag handy to clean off your finger.

Apply grout sealer to the joints with a small paintbrush and let it soak in. Make sure to wipe excess sealer off the tiles before it dries.

MAINTENANCE and REPAIR

People choose ceramic tile for its durability as well as its beauty. It's one of the easiest building materials to keep clean – even the grout joints can be kept fresh-looking for years with a little annual maintenance.

When tile is properly installed, most repair jobs are routine. Over the life of a project you may need to replace a loose or cracked tile or two, or replace grout that has become worn or stained. In addition, you may need to recaulk joints to keep water from seeping beneath the tile. To save time and money, try to take care of problems as they arise. Postponing repairs just makes the job harder and, in the long run, more expensive.

Maintenance

Wipe up spills immediately and clean tile regularly to prevent dirt and grime from building up. For cleaning, use the products recommended by the manufacturer. Hot water and an all-purpose household cleaner work fine to remove light to medium grime – just rinse the tiles well after washing to remove any detergent film. Some tile retailers and home centers sell special tile cleaners, but read the labels on these carefully and use them exactly as recommended, since some may etch the tile glaze if they're left on too long. Never use harsh, abrasive cleaners, such as scouring powder, on ceramic tiles because they could damage the glaze, too. It's best to avoid using colored cleaners on unglazed tile and grout because the dyes in the cleaner may stain.

Clean grout joints regularly with a stiff brush and a commercial non-bleach household cleaner. While you can use bleach to clean stains and mildew from white grout, never use bleach on colored grouts. (You can also use commercial grout cleaners, but since these may actually remove some of the grout from the joints, don't use them more than once a year.) Test your cleaner in an inconspicuous area before use to make sure it won't fade the grout color. Reseal the grout after you clean it to prevent stains from soaking in. Most sealer manufacturers recommend an annual application of grout sealer.

Scrub the grout with a small stiff-bristled brush and all-purpose household cleaner or grout cleaner. Tile cleaners that claim to remove mildew sometimes contain bleach – read labels carefully and test the cleaner in an inconspicuous area to make sure it won't discolor the grout joints.

Clean off hard-water spots and film with a plastic scouring pad and either household cleaner or a mixture of white vinegar and water. Rinse the tiles thoroughly after washing and dry them with a soft cloth.

Apply grout sealer once a year. On glazed tiles, wipe off any drips before they have a chance to dry. If the tiles are unglazed, mask both sides of the grout joint to prevent the sealer from staining the tiles.

Troubleshooting

Ceramic tiles and the grout joints between them may crack for a variety of reasons. Many times the reason for the damage is obvious (for example, when tiles break from the impact of a heavy object). Other times damaged tiles and grout are a sign that something is fundamentally wrong with the installation. Before making any repairs, it's important to diagnose – and correct – any underlying problems. Otherwise, your tile and grout will continue to need repair no matter how many times you replace them.

Grout problems

Typically, grout joints crack because of improper installation. A too-flexible underlayment is a major culprit, as is poor adhesion between the tiles and the underlayment (as the tiles loosen in their setting bed, they pull the grout joints apart). Also, if the grout wasn't thoroughly packed into the joints during installation, the air pockets left behind could result in flaking and cracking.

Trouble with tile

The cause of tile problems can range from the simple (ordinary hard use) to the complex (shifting or settling of the foundation). Common problems include an uneven underlayment and improper installation. For example, where cracks appear in one area of a large floor, it may indicate the lack of an expansion joint between the wall and the floor. The tiles crack when the wall and floor move with seasonal changes in humidity and take the tiles with them. One or two cracked tiles in a floor or wall are probably nothing to worry about, but large sections of cracking can be a sign of a structural problem with the house.

Tiles loosen most often on walls and floors in wet areas. When water gets behind the tile, the moisture weakens the adhesive, causing it to lose its grip on the tile. Using the wrong adhesive or one that has been incorrectly mixed can also cause tiles to loosen over time, as can excessive vibrations, such as those caused by slamming doors.

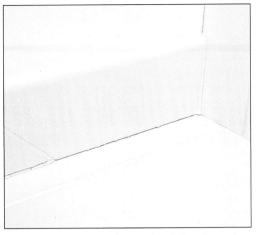

This grout joint was doomed to failure from the beginning because of its location – at the junction of two perpendicular surfaces. In a case like this, dig out the grout and caulk the joint instead.

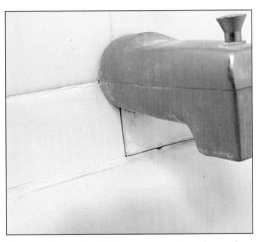

Cracked grout will let water seep into the underlayment beneath the tile. If the underlayment here is drywall, it will likely be damaged and need replacing (with backer board, not more drywall).

Remove mildew and stains from grout with a small, stiff brush and a tile cleaner designed for the purpose. Let the grout dry thoroughly before coating it with a sealer.

If you're lucky, you can cut out the old caulk with a utility knife. The new joint will last longer if you remove as much of the old caulk as possible.

Stubborn caulk is easier to remove if you warm it first with a heat gun. Once the caulk softens, dig it out with a utility knife.

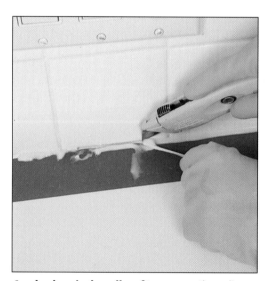

Apply chemical caulk softener exactly as directed on the label. Usually you will have to let it stand a bit before scraping out the caulk with a utility knife. Protect adjacent surfaces from the chemicals in the softener.

Recaulking

Good tub-and-tile caulk stays flexible – and watertight – for years, so you probably won't have to recaulk very often. If you do notice cracks or gaps in a caulk joint, take care of the problem immediately, since any water that gets behind the tiles can damage the underlayment. While it may be tempting to smear a little new caulk into the damaged areas, this won't give you the continuous watertight seal that's needed. The repair will be much more effective and durable if you dig out the old caulk before applying the new.

Repairing a damaged caulk joint is easy. You cut out the old caulk with a utility knife, clean the debris out of the joint, then wipe off any soap residue with a little rubbing alcohol on a clean cloth. Let the area dry for several minutes before applying the new caulk. You can either push the gun along the joint or pull it, just keep the joint continuous. After the joint is full, immediately smooth the caulk with your finger.

Apply a fresh bead of caulk, squeezing the caulk-gun trigger slowly and steadily as you move along the joint. Immediately smooth the caulk with a wet finger, then peel off the masking tape.

Regrouting

Grout is porous and absorbs water. As a result, it can flake, crack, and get moldy. If the damage is limited, you can clean out just the area needing repair. If the grout has large, dirty cracks, you'll have to remove all or most of the old grout and replace it with fresh grout. The best way to remove grout from a joint is with a grout saw. There are two types: one with a sharp serrated carbide-steel blade, the other with an abrasive blade.

Grout comes in a variety of colors, so make sure the new grout matches the color of the existing grout. For small areas, it's easier to use premixed grout (which comes in small containers or tubes) instead of powdered grout, but it may be harder to find a matching color.

Dig out the old grout with a grout saw. Cut down to sound grout and then a little beyond, just to make sure you've removed all of the damaged grout and that there's room for the new grout.

Pick out loose chunks that have gotten wedged into the joint with a small, sharp tool such as a nut pick or nail. Don't chip off solid grout at the edges of the joint – it can result in a chipped tile.

Brush or vacuum out all the debris after cleaning out the joint. Remove any dirt, oil, or soap scum with bathroom cleaner or rubbing alcohol.

Apply the new grout after the joint has dried. For small areas, it's convenient to use a small squeeze tube of premixed grout, provided you can find the matching color. To regrout large areas, use the techniques described in chapter 7.

Replacing a Tile

The hardest part of replacing a broken tile is removing it without breaking any more tiles. Your best bet is to remove as much of the grout around the tile as possible before chipping out the damaged tile.

If you're replacing a group of tiles, try to set them with the same type of adhesive as the original tiles. If you're replacing just one tile, you can use a silicone adhesive. After pressing the tile in place, clean up any adhesive that oozes through the joints. If you're replacing tile on a wall, tape it into place until it dries. Let the adhesive set up for the recommended amount of time before grouting.

Remove grout *around the damaged tile with a grout saw. If you skip this step, you could break adjoining tiles when removing the broken one. For a group of tiles, dig out the grout around the section of tiles you're replacing.*

Shatter the broken tile *into small pieces by hitting it with a hammer and a punch. Make sure to wear your safety glasses to protect your eyes from flying chips. Carefully pry out the pieces.*

Scrape off all the old adhesive *with a chisel or a putty knife. If the underlayment is drywall, be careful not to dig into it. Get the surface as clean as possible.*

Apply adhesive *to the back of the tile and set it in place. Be careful not to put on too much or too little adhesive – you want the new tile to sit level with the rest of the tiles.*

CERAMIC TILE PROJECTS

While kitchens and bathrooms come to mind most often when people think of ceramic tile, there are plenty of other places where tile can be used creatively. Some of the projects shown here require more time and know-how than others – you may even need to hire out part of the job to a professional. Other projects just require extra-careful planning and attention to detail, and perhaps some practice at a new skill, such as laying out tiles in a diagonal pattern. But all the projects shown here, whether they're on a large scale or a small one, are alike in that they let you take full advantage of the decorative value of tile both inside and outside your home.

Stone Floors

Natural stone floors are both beautiful and durable. You can choose among rugged rough-hewn stone, tumbled stone tiles, and more formal polished stone tiles. Rough-hewn stone is irregularly shaped and sized. Stone tiles are flat and most are trimmed into squares ranging from 4 inches to 24 inches.

To prevent stains from soaking in, all stone tiles should be finished with a sealer especially formulated for stone. Typically, this is done after grouting, but it's a good idea to seal rough-hewn stone before grouting. If left unsealed, its porous surface is more likely to absorb grout, resulting in a dull, foggy appearance. It's also more likely to stain during regular use. Rough-hewn stone doesn't seal as well as stone tiles, so it's not a good choice for areas that will have direct contact with water.

Rough-hewn stone comes in uneven shapes that have to be carefully fitted together. It's best used for informal settings. Keep small, thin pieces of stone handy to shim furniture on the uneven top surface of the stone.

1 **Dry-fit the stones** before installing them. You'll have to split some stones with a stone chisel and a hammer to make them fit. While there is bound to be some fluctuation in joint width, try to make sure joint size stays fairly consistent throughout the project.

2 **Set each stone** in place after spreading thinset mortar onto the subfloor and combing it into ridges. Because of the uneven surfaces and thicknesses of the stones, you can expect to adjust the amount of mortar under each stone to level it.

4 **Use a grout bag** to grout the joints between stones. The grout bag will help keep the grout in the joints and off the surface of unfinished stones, where it could penetrate the porous surface of the stone and result in a cloudy appearance.

3 **Make sure** each stone is sitting at the same height as the stones adjacent to it. For accuracy, run the level across several stones. Adjust the amount of mortar under the stones as necessary.

5 **Smooth** the joints with a pointing trowel after the grout has hardened a little. Compact the grout around the edges of the stones. If some grout gets on the stone, wait for it to dry then sweep it away with a whisk broom – don't try to scrub it off with a wet brush or rag.

Setting rough-hewn stone

Because rough-hewn stones vary in thickness and come in irregular shapes, fitting them together is a matter of trial and error. Aim for an even distribution of sizes, splitting pieces as necessary to fit them into the pattern. As you set each stone, make sure it's level with adjacent stones. After letting the mortar set up, fill the joints between stones with grout. Because of the rough texture and porous surface of the stone, you'll have to apply the grout with a grout bag instead of a float. Mix the grout just wet enough to flow through the tip of the bag. While additional water weakens the grout a little, the joints will still be sturdy enough to endure normal use.

Setting stone tile

Because there's practically no grout joint to help hide slight variations in height, stone tiles must be set perfectly flat. The tiles tend to vary slightly in thickness, so you'll have to adjust the amount of mortar underneath many of the tiles. For the best bond, make sure to use the adhesive recommended by the manufacturer – not all adhesives are compatible with all types of stone. Because the stone can absorb the adhesive, use light thinset for light-colored stone, dark thinset for dark stone. Stone tiles are dense, so you'll have to cut them with a wet saw. Clean dust and any manufacturer's residue off the backs of stone tiles before setting them into the thinset. Because they are typically polished, stone tiles can be grouted with a grout float rather than a grout bag. A sealer is typically applied after the stone tiles have been grouted.

Stone tile gives a room warmth and richness. The symmetrical shapes and sizes make it more suitable for formal settings than rough-hewn stone. Typically the grout joints between polished stone tiles are very narrow.

1 **Stone tiles** require precise placement because of the narrow joints. Drop – don't slide – the tile directly in place in the combed thinset mortar.

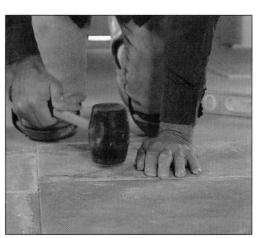

2 **Professional tilesetters** will sometimes use a lift knob (a suction-cup device) to set stone tiles and to lift them up when it's necessary to adjust the amount of mortar underneath.

3 **Beat in each tile** to level it and to ensure a good bond with the thinset. Although stone tile is dimensioned, there are slight variations in size from tile to tile.

Diagonal Tile Patterns

Tiles can be set in a variety of patterns or on the diagonal for any number of custom looks. Diagonally set tiles look attractive, but it can be a real challenge to lay out an entire wall of diagonal tiles and come up with symmetrical cut tiles around the perimeter of the installation.

A project using diagonal tiles can be considerably simplified if you lay out an area of diagonal tiles within a border of straight tiles; this allows you to design the size of the diagonal area to accommodate half-tiles around the perimeter.

In the design shown here, half-tiles fit between the diagonal full tiles around the entire perimeter of the frame. A pattern like this still requires a lot of cutting, and if the tiles have a directional pattern or grain, you'll need to orient the tiles during cutting so the pattern or grain will match that of the full tiles. You're bound to break more than a few tiles when cutting diagonals, so make sure to buy extra tiles to cover the breakage.

Although tiles are set the same way whether they're positioned in decorative or simple patterns, the layout of a patterned project can require more painstaking labor to make the job come out right. With a diagonal pattern, try to keep the cut tiles symmetrical

The frame of diagonal tiles centered over the bathtub is the focal point in this bathroom. The diagonal tiles are separated from the field tiles with a border of narrow trim tiles of a slightly darker color.

1 *Eyeball the joints between tiles* and adjust them as needed before moving on to the next section. Note that the border and field tiles are being set simultaneously. Drawing a precise grid of reference lines for each part of the pattern will keep the installation on track.

across the layout. Remember, there is no one right way to lay out the tile – just keep experimenting until you come up with a layout you like.

When you're satisfied with the layout, use a level or a framing square to draw reference lines on the backer board. In addition to the main vertical and horizontal reference lines, you should draw some diagonal reference lines. These should be at a 45-degree angle to the vertical and horizontal lines. To position the 45-degree lines, first draw a line between an end of the horizontal reference line and an end of the vertical line. Bisect this line, then draw another line from that point down to the intersection of the horizontal and vertical reference lines. On a patterned wall, it's also important to mark a perfectly level horizontal reference line around the whole space.

It's the only way to be sure that the horizontal grout joints will match up in each corner.

When laying out shaped tiles, like hexagons or octagons, use the straight sides of the tile or the pointed tips as reference points to orient the tiles within the grid of layout lines. Customize the grid as necessary to make sure you have sufficient reference points. Odd-shaped tiles are harder to position on the layout grid, but you can still use any consistent part of the design – such as a tile's pointed ends or the halfway point of the tile's length – for reference. Odd-shaped tiles, unlike square or rectangular tiles, will overlap the reference lines so you'll have to pay extra attention when setting the tiles to make sure they're positioned properly in the grid. Use a straightedge as necessary to orient the tiles to the reference lines.

2 **Work one section** of the grid at a time. Here the tiles are being set along the upper reference line.

3 **Set the field** and border tiles first, then go back and fill in the tiles outside the border.

The jig is up

The hardest part about making diagonal cuts is keeping them consistent. That's where a jig comes in handy. The jig holds the tile so the cut runs perfectly straight from corner to corner. Jigs are available for many snap cutters and wet saws, but if you can't find one, you can make your own. The plywood jig shown here sits on the sliding table of a wet saw. One side of the jig has a plywood V screwed to the plywood base; the V holds the tile in place. The other piece of plywood is just to keep the tile level. To make a straight cut, just lift the jig off the saw table.

Custom Shower Stall

Tiling a shower stall is basically the same as tiling any other wall. Because shower walls are regularly splashed with water, you'll have to make the installation as moisture resistant as possible. And, unless you're an experienced tilesetter, you should select a preformed shower pan. Your options include solid-surface, fiberglass, and acrylic shower pans. If you want a ceramic tile floor in the shower, you need a mortar pan. Pouring a mortar pan is a job to leave to a professional tilesetter.

Installing the shower pan

Typically, the framing for a shower enclosure is sized so that the shower pan will just fit inside. It can be a little difficult to maneuver the pan in and out of the opening for test-fitting and installation. Once the pan is in place, it's easy to secure it – simply attach the pan to the studs through the top lip. Before getting to this point, however, consider two very important issues. First, the pan unit must remain rigid. If your floor isn't smooth or if your pan is flimsy, you may need to set the pan on top of a layer of mortar or concrete so the pan won't flex or bend. Second, it's essential that the drain pipe be exactly centered in the hole in the bottom of the shower pan. Otherwise you may not get a tight seal between the pipe and the drain hardware. To avoid leaks, make sure the drain assembly fits the drain pipe snugly. If necessary, use a hammer to tap down the gasket that came with the assembly. Use a wood shim to protect the gasket from damage.

1 *Cut* the shower pan stub-out to the correct height with a handsaw. To figure out the height, test-fit the pan and mark the height of the cut on the drain pipe.

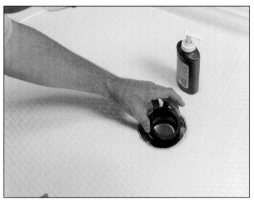

2 *Fit the drain assembly* to the drain pipe. The assembly comes with a gasket that seals it to the pipe. It's a tight fit – use some liquid soap to lubricate the fitting and help it slide into place.

3 *Frame out* between studs to make a shampoo niche. Attach backer board to the drywall at the back of the niche with silicone adhesive (not fasteners). Nail or screw strips of backer board to the niche framing.

4 *Draw a series of reference lines* to guide your installation. In a shower installation, the grout lines between walls and ceiling should match. Start with the centerline, then add parallel and perpendicular lines as needed.

Cover the shower pan with a drop cloth to protect it until you're done installing the backer board and tile.

Underlayment

Backer board is the best choice of underlayment for a shower stall. The backer board should overlap the lip of the shower pan, but stop ¼ inch short of the edge of the shower pan. (Later on you'll run a bead of caulk in the gap to create a durable, waterproof seal.) Depending on how thick the lip of the pan is, you may have to fur out the studs in order to slip the backer board over the lip. If you're framing out a niche to hold bath products, line the niche walls and back with backer board, too. After you mud and tape the joints, spread some liquid isolation membrane in the niche to keep water from leaking inside the wall (the isolation membrane also serves as a waterproofer).

Tile layout

When you're tiling the ceiling (or as the pros say, tiling the lid), laying out a tile job can get tricky. Since the grout lines on the walls must line up with the grout lines on the ceiling, layout becomes like a three-dimensional tic-tac-toe game – what you do on one wall affects the layout of another wall. The close quarters of a shower stall will magnify any grout joints that are misaligned – a little extra time spent now will be well worth the investment.

Concentrate on keeping full tiles at the most visible areas of the installation and avoiding cut tiles narrower than a half-tile

5 *Measure the walls* to determine the best placement of the tiles within the shower surround. The outside edges (room side) of the surround are highly visible, so you want to plan on full tiles there.

6 *Check how the tiles* will fall in corners and at special features, such as the shampoo niche. Whenever it's possible, adjust the layout to avoid narrow cuts.

7 *Firmly press* the ceiling tiles into place. The tiles seen here come joined together in sheets with rubber dots. The dots hold the tiles exactly the right distance apart, so you just have to get the spacing right from sheet to sheet. Bullnose tiles finish off the front edge.

8 ***Place small shims*** *of scrap tile in the corner to angle the bench slightly so water will drain off.*

9 ***Set the shower seat*** *with silicone adhesive. The tiles below help support the seat. Note how the tiles below the seat were trimmed to allow the top of the bench to fall in the grout line.*

wide. Draw a center line across the ceiling and down the back wall. Then, start playing with the layout of the wall tile (p. 50). Draw a grid of layout lines and transfer them across the ceiling. Plan to use bullnose tiles to finish off the edges of the shower enclosure.

Setting the tile

If you're tiling the lid, start your tilesetting there. It's easier than you think to set tile on the ceiling. Mastic grips the tiles quickly, so you aren't too likely to get bonked on the head with a falling tile. Spread only one grid section at a time with adhesive and lay the tile there before moving on to the next section.

Tile the shower enclosure in sections, too, finishing one wall before moving on to another. Sheet-mounted tiles speed up installation because the small tiles within each sheet are pre-spaced. You set them the same way you set single wall tiles. Rubber-dot and mesh backings are left in place when the tile sheet is placed in the adhesive. If you're using sheet-mounted tiles with a paper facing, the tiles are set into the adhesive and then the paper is dampened and scrubbed off after the adhesive has set.

As soon as you've finished installing a section of tile, clean out any adhesive that oozes up in the grout joints or onto the surfaces of the tile. Be careful not to knock any tiles out of alignment.

10 ***The two tiles*** *that go around the ends of the seat must fit tightly against the seat to help hold it in place. Remove a tile from the sheet, notch it to size, then press it firmly into the adhesive.*

11 ***The tiles above the seat*** *lock it into place. The border tiles shown here are sheet mounted in a stock pattern available from the manufacturer. Even a detail as simple as this can add a custom look to otherwise plain walls.*

The wet wall (the wall with the plumbing stub-outs) can be challenging because sometimes you'll have to make curved cuts. Much of the time, a simple notch will do (especially when the cut tile will be covered by an escutcheon plate). When working around plumbing stub-outs, try to avoid splitting the tile in half and trimming a half-hole on the cut edge of each tile. The resulting joint won't be wide enough for grout or caulk, so it will be easy for water to seep in and do some damage.

Special features

A seat or bench makes the shower more comfortable and safer to use. It should be at least 12 inches deep and be placed about 14 to 18 inches above the floor, depending on the height of the people who will be using the shower. The shower seat shown here is a triangle of ¾-inch solid-surface material. It's glued to the backer board with silicone adhesive and locked in place by the rows of tile above and below it. You can buy smaller triangles of solid-surface material and install them the same way to make shelves in the shower.

The shelf in the shampoo niche is also made of solid-surface material. Because it has no seams, there's no chance for water to seep through it and get behind the wall. Still, the joints along the sides and back of the shelf are vulnerable to water, so angle the shelf slightly downward for drainage.

12 ***Back-butter*** *the shelf for the shower niche and set it into place. It's angled slightly, like the shower bench, to allow water to run off.*

13 ***Space is tight*** *inside the niche, so you may want to back-butter these tiles. The side tiles are bullnosed to cap the corner between the niche and the wall.*

14 ***Notch tiles*** *as necessary to fit around the showerhead and faucets. The escutcheon plate will cover the cut in this tile so it's okay if the cut is a little rough.*

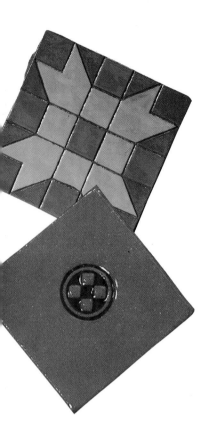

Grouting

You can begin to grout the shower enclosure about 24 hours after completing the tilesetting. Mask off the shower pan to protect it from being damaged by the grout. Working with small amounts of grout will keep the mess to a minimum when you grout the ceiling, but wear long sleeves and safety glasses just in case.

Make sure to get all the dust and debris out of the joints before applying the grout. (See chapter 7 for more on grouting.) After the grout has cured, caulk the joints anywhere two different materials meet and anywhere tile meets tile in two different planes. Finish up the job by applying grout sealer according to the manufacturer's directions.

15 *Grout the ceiling of the shower enclosure first, packing the grout into the joints. Stand on a ladder if necessary – your arms will tire less rapidly if they're not stretched to the max.*

16 *To grout the shower niche, use the smallest possible float you can find. Move the float across the tiles to force the grout into the joints.*

17 *Caulk the joints where walls meet, at the top edge of the shower pan, around the shower bench, and anyplace where two different types of materials come together. For a neat caulk job, mask both sides of the joint and run the caulk in between.*

Mosaic Floor

Many mosaic tiles are available mounted on sheets so you can install them in larger sections. Stock designs are readily available in sheet-mounted mosaic tiles. You can also have a custom design sheet mounted, but it'll cost you. Setting small mosaic tiles is a time-consuming job; many people choose to hire professional tilesetters to install complicated mosaics.

Installing a complex pattern like this one can take a long time if you can work on it only in your spare time, as this contractor has. To protect the areas he's set, he grouts each section once the thinset has cured.

Spread thinset over just a small area at a time, otherwise it will skin over before you can set all the tiles (a margin trowel works fine for this). Then back-butter each tile by dipping it in thinset before setting it.

Fireplace Surround

Check with your building department before you tile a fireplace surround since, depending on the installation, local codes often have specific requirements regarding clearance and underlayment issues. Fireplaces (and woodstoves) throw off a lot of heat so it's important to use the right adhesive for setting the tile. Stay away from all types of organic mastic because heat can cause the adhesive bond to fail. Instead, choose a heat-resistant thinset mortar (some thinsets can endure temperatures up to 400 degrees). The setting surface must be absolutely free of soot and dirt or the adhesive won't bond well.

1 **To avoid getting** adhesive on the fireplace insert, hold back the thinset from the bottom edge. Back-butter the corresponding edge of each piece before setting it.

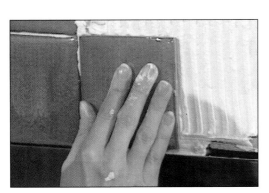

2 **Set each tile in place** with a slight twist. Note how no thinset was troweled near the fireplace insert (lower right).

3 **After cleaning off** the bulk of the excess grout, remove the grout haze with a clean sponge as soon as it appears.

1 *Arrange the tiles* in a test run on each stair tread. Make sure you're satisfied with the pattern before you start setting the tiles.

3 *Use a margin trowel* to load thinset onto the notched trowel, then spread the thinset over the riser. In this project, a polymer-fortified thinset adhesive was used because the tile was set right on the wood risers.

Stair Risers

Covering stair risers with tile is an easy way to add stunning detail to an ordinary staircase. There's a safety benefit, too: Risers that contrast with the treads can make it easier to see the stairs when the light is dim.

In some cases you'll be able to find tiles that fit your risers exactly. In other cases, it will be necessary to lay out a design using different sizes of tile. One pattern that often works is a center row of full 4-inch tiles with a row of cut tiles on the top and bottom. (A benefit of this arrangement is that it helps disguise out-of-square risers.)

You typically won't need many tiles, so a stairway is a great place to use special or handmade tiles, since you can get maximum decorative impact for minimum cost. But be careful when selecting a pattern – small patterns can look busy, while large patterns can lack impact.

2 *Draw the reference lines.* The first line here was marked dead center, then lines were marked to indicate the top and bottom of the full tiles. Measure from these lines to the top and bottom of the riser to determine the size of the cut tiles.

4 *Comb the thinset* into ridges. Cover the stair treads to protect them from adhesive drips.

5 **Start setting tile** at the center of the riser if you have a pattern that must be centered. Note the pencil marks at the back edge of the tread; transferring the marks to the treads gives you a reference point once the lines on the risers get covered up.

6 **Grout the joints** about 24 hours after setting the tile. Protect adjoining surfaces with masking tape. If you have a hard time getting enough grout into the corners, smear some on with your hand, then work it with the grout float.

Installation

If your stairs allow, add a ¼-inch layer of backer board to each riser to make the project more durable. This is preferable to tiling on wood, which expands and contracts with changes in humidity. The movement of the wood can cause grout joints and tiles to crack. Use polymer-fortified thinset and grout to help compensate for the movement of a wood substrate.

If using more than one row of tile per riser, start with the bottom tile first, then work up to the top; this will prevent the top tiles from sliding down in the adhesive and will hide any unevenness under the treads. When tiling such a small space, it's easiest to cut all the cut tiles needed before you start tiling. That way you can apply thinset to the entire riser, set all the tiles, adjust the spacing of the tiles as needed, then move on to the next riser.

7 **Caulk the joints** at all four sides after the grout has cured. Before caulking, replace the masking tape with some fresh tape. Otherwise, dust and little chunks of grout may get into the caulk.

8 **Peel off the masking tape** once the caulk has firmed up. If using unglazed tiles, consider sealing the tiles and grout to protect them from wear and tear.

Tiling a Table

If you're not up for a big ceramic tile job, a tiled tabletop is the perfect weekend project. Tiles can be arranged in a variety of decorative patterns to cover a coffee or end table, or in a checkerboard pattern to top a gaming table. Tables – not the kitchen floor – are the place to go wild with colors and patterns.

You can make a frame for your table or, even easier, buy a table at a home decorating center and discard or tile over the top. Flea markets and garage sales often offer solid, inexpensive tables that are good for tiling. Before you tile a table, make sure the frame is sound and the joints are strong. Tiles are heavy, and a rickety table won't be able to support the weight of the tiled tabletop.

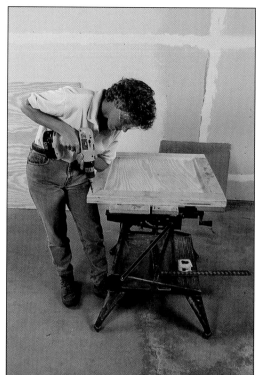

1 ***Assemble a base*** *of ¾-inch plywood topped with ½-inch backer board. To avoid cutting tiles, you can size the top to accommodate full tiles and the grout joints between them. Here, adding ¾-inch plywood strips around the edges allows the use of full 2-inch tiles on the edges.*

2 ***Draw reference lines*** *on the base with a framing square. In this case the pattern is a checkerboard and it is important to center it on the table surface.*

3 ***Thinset mortar*** *is a good adhesive for tabletops because they're subject to spills and moisture from sweating glasses.*

4 ***A jig holds the tile*** *in position for a diagonal cut. On a project as small as this one it's best to make all the cuts at once.*

Tiles

Tiles with softly rounded edges work well for tabletops, but you could also use regular field tiles for the center and bullnose tiles around the perimeter of the table. Use either bullnose or square-edged tiles to cover the edges of the base. The tiles should come together flush where the edge meets the table surface. If the perimeter tiles on the tabletop overhang the edge tiles, the tiles can easily chip or be popped off by things catching on the lip.

Grouting

Small projects like this offer a good excuse to experiment with colored grouts. One word of warning: When using a colored grout, make sure to clean the all the excess thinset out of the joints. If globs of thinset remain in the joints and you grout over them, the color may be different in those places than where the grout goes all the way to the bottom of the joint.

5 **Set the border tiles** once all the field tiles are in place. Mixing in a few 4-inch tiles and a few diagonal cuts punches up the design without adding much to the cost.

6 **Tile the edges** of the tabletop after the top tiles have set overnight. Attach the tiles with silicone adhesive instead of thinset mortar. Use strips of masking tape to secure the tiles until the adhesive has cured.

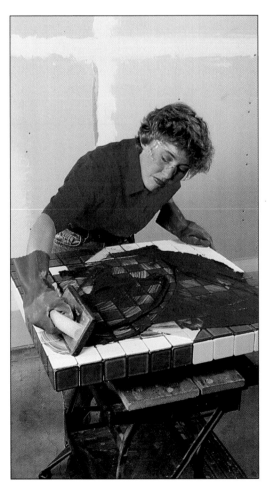

7 **Float the grout** onto the tabletop, forcing the grout into the joints with a diagonal motion, then remove the excess grout and the grout haze.

8 **If you use the table outside,** bring it in during the cold months to prevent cracking.

Tiling a Patio

The primary consideration for a tiled patio is slab condition. Cracks and low spots can be repaired, but if the slab is in bad shape, you'll have to resurface it before proceeding. What's more, the patio should slope about one inch per every 4 to 8 feet to encourage rain to drain off. This will help prevent damage to the patio during cold weather, when trapped water could freeze and heave the tiles. If your patio isn't sloped, consider mudjacking the patio or resurfacing the patio with concrete to create a slope before tiling. Don't try to create the necessary slope by adding thinset when you set the tile.

Be careful in your choice of tiles for outdoor use, especially in cold areas where the tile will have to endure freeze/thaw cycles. Vitreous tiles are recommended; because they aren't porous they absorb practically no water. If you're using quarry tile for a patio,

1 *The best base* for a tiled patio is a concrete slab. Before tiling, clean any dirt and debris off the slab and scrub it with a degreaser.

2 *Use a level* to determine the slope of the slab. The slab should slope about an inch over every 4 to 8 feet to ensure that water will run off rather than puddle. Also inspect the slab for overall condition – you'll have to fill major cracks and holes before tiling.

3 *Grind off high spots* on the slab with a grinder. For small bumps, you can use a hammer and a chisel.

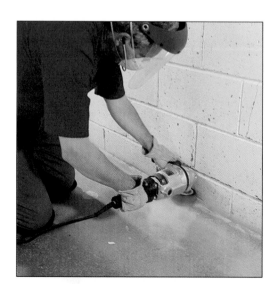

4 *Plan your layout carefully.* If the tiles will be set in a pattern, lay out some tiles to determine the best positions for the reference lines. Here it worked out that the end of a tile would fall exactly every 2 feet along the edge of the patio, so that's where the lines were snapped.

make sure to select the vitreous type, since quarry tile is also available in semi-vitreous form. Quarry tile works well for patios because it's unglazed and less slippery when wet. For durability in outdoor jobs, use latex-fortified thinset and grout.

Laying out a patio is not very different from laying out other tile jobs. You want to make sure that the pattern looks good and that any cut pieces are at least half a tile wide. Measure the length and width of the patio and dry-fit the tiles to figure out the layout. Adjust the layout if necessary by shifting tiles, then decide where you want to start setting the tiles.

Mix the thinset and let it slake as directed. Apply it within the grid lines using a square-notched trowel. Mix and spread only enough thinset to cover a few grid sections at a time. Otherwise, the thinset will dry out, which makes it not only harder to spread, but weakens the bond between it and the tile.

5 *Snap a grid* of reference lines after double-checking how the tiles will fall at each edge of the slab.

6 *By back-buttering* the portion of the tile that falls outside the grid line, you can avoid covering up grid lines with adhesive.

7 *Quarry tiles* can be cut with either a snap cutter or a wet saw. In this project, half-tiles were required at the edges and other cut tiles were needed to fit around obstructions.

8 *A job like this* goes pretty fast with two people – one mixing thinset and cutting tile, the other spreading thinset and setting tile. But if you have to stop midway, clean up and cover the whole patio with a sheet of plastic to protect the site from dirt and rain.

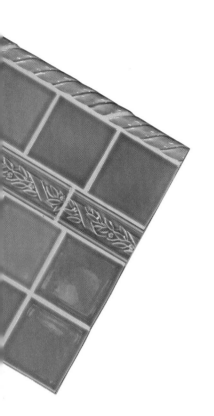

For outdoor use, mix the grout with an acrylic additive instead of water. Apply the grout in small sections. Move the grout float diagonally across the joints to force the grout between the tiles, then scrape up the excess grout with the float before moving on to the next section. Wait 10 to 15 minutes to let the joints firm up a bit, then sponge off as much grout as possible from the tiles. Polish off the grout haze as soon as it becomes visible. If you let the haze sit, it will become more difficult to remove. Caulk any joints between the patio and the house or garage with a polyurethane caulk that matches the color of the grout.

9 **Apply the grout** *after the thinset has cured overnight. Work in small sections. (See chapter 7 for more about grouting).*

Easy release

Grout mixed with additives is notorious for leaving behind a hard-to-remove haze. To test if this will be a problem with your job, mix up a small batch of grout and smear a little across some sample tiles. If it looks like there is going to be a problem, you can apply a grout release product before grouting. Test the grout release on a sample tile to make sure it won't change the color of the tile. Apply the grout release only to the tile faces, not to the edges, because it will affect the bond of the grout to the tile sides. Another way to cut down on problems with haze is to seal the tiles before grouting.

If haze has dried on the tile, first try to remove it with plain water and a white plastic scrubbing pad. If that doesn't work, try a solution of white vinegar and water or ask the grout manufacturer to recommend a haze removing product.

10 **A quick way to apply** *tile sealer is with a garden sprayer or paint roller. Let the sealer set for about 10 minutes, then blot the excess with a rag.*

Index